AF346178

What people are saying about this book...

"A captivating book from cover to cover, and what's best is that the whole story is told in its historical, social, religious, and political context."
Le Courrier de l'Ouest

"A poignant story from Viviane Janouin-Benanti"
Vendée Matin

"If there is one thread that connects all of Viviane Janouin-Benanti's works, it's that she chooses to side with the victims..."
L'Écho de la Presqu'île

"An absolutely captivating investigative piece..."
Ouest France

"Viviane Janouin-Benanti's novels revive an old French tradition: retelling the stories of criminal cases."
Review by Delphine Cignal on *Lycos*

"This sad story, narrated like a novel, reveals the divisions that plagued provincial society..."
Review by Paul Maugendre, *Les Lectures de l'Oncle Paul*

"A brilliantly conducted investigation, well documented and easy to read."
Historia

"The author's lively style takes this horrifying true story to a new level."
Lire en Vendée

The PoitiersAffair

A Harrowing True Crime Story

Viviane Janouin-Benanti

The Poitiers Affair

A Harrowing True Crime Story

Translated by Elizabeth Blood

3E éditions

Collection: Crime Novels
Cover Design: *3E* éditions
ISBN : 978-2-37885-059-3

PREFACE

Look closely at this photo.

It was taken in the hospital just after Blanche was rescued, and the doctors who examined her determined that she had been saved just in time.

I found this photo profoundly shocking when I first saw it while in law school. Still today, I can't look at it without emotion, without compassion. I promised myself then that one day I would tell this woman's story.

It is important that people know what she had to endure, how much she suffered to end up like this.

This story takes place in the 19th century in the small city of Poitiers, located 338 kilometers (210 miles) south-west of Paris in what is today the Nouvelle-Aquitaine region of France. For almost a century after the French Revolution, France struggled with political instability, switching from the First Republic (1792–1804), to the Empire of Napoléon I (1804–1815), to the Restoration of the Bourbon monarchy (1815–1830), to another revolution and a new king Louis-Philippe (1830–1848), to yet another revolution and the establishment of a Second Republic (1848–1852), to a coup d'état that led to the Second Empire of Napoléon III (1852–1870), and finally to a Third Republic (1870–1940) marked by a violent socialist insurrection called the Paris Commune (1871). It was a society fraught with ongoing rivalries between the *Républicain* left, the *Royaliste* right, the socialist workers' party, and those who still fondly longed for another Bonaparte emperor. Also in the mix were social class distinctions and continued rifts between Catholics and Protestants. While Poitiers was removed from the violent clashes happening in Paris, the political drama played out in this provincial capital on a personal level in the form of enmity, jealousy, fear, prejudice, obsession, and mistrust among neighbors and compatriots. Blanche was an unfortunate victim of this drama, hidden away, abused, and neglected almost to the point of no return.

Her alarming case drew attention from all corners of France, and made a particular impact on people in Paris where all of the emotions that this case evoked were expressed in popular illustrations and songs. Indeed, the response was so strong that the "captive of Poitiers" never really disappeared from collective memory in France. The famous author André Gide wrote a summary of the trial in 1930, and the two court rulings related to the case are still studied in law schools in France and other French-speaking countries.

To get to know her better, to understand what happened, I consulted as many sources as possible. I pored over all of the articles that came out at that time. I read national newspapers representing the widest possible array of political opinions: *L'Éclair*, *l'Illustration*, *La Croix*, *La Libre Parole*, *L'Écho de Paris*, *l'Univers*, *Le Petit Journal*. I was able to read the court records of the trial and various witness testimonies. Although intended to prove the innocence of Blanche's brother, of particular interest are the observations made by the defense attorney, Maître Barbier, as he spoke before the Indictments Chamber of the Court of Appeals in Poitiers.

The regional press was obviously most interested in the case. There were, in particular, two newspapers in Poitiers with opposing political views: the conservative Royalist newspaper *Le Courrier de la Vienne et des Deux-Sèvres* and the voice of the French *Républicains* who favored a democratic republic, *L'Avenir de la Vienne*.

The newspapers of this era are a treasure trove of information. They reveal in detail every aspect of the case. And, in general, the reporters did try to be objective and present the facts, all except for the Royalist newspapers like *Le Courrier de la Vienne et des Deux-Sèvres*. From the start, and before knowing even the most basic facts about what happened, this paper sided with Blanche's mother, one of Poitiers' most notable and most notorious *Royalistes*.

This brings us to another peculiarity of this case: the heated controversies surrounding the trial. The deep divisions between political groups like the Royalists, the Bonapartists, the anti-clericals, and the *Républicains*, as well as the disparities between the upper classes and the working classes, often led to facts being perverted in order to prove the innocence or the guilt of Blanche's family members. A few people, like the Catholic priest Father Mondion and a small number of serious journalists, were able to stick to the facts and tell Blanche's story with the humanity and objectivity it deserved. It is particularly interesting to note that 100 years later one still encounters vestiges of these divisions whenever the Poitiers Affair is brought up in conversation.

I

February 16, 1847: A trial in Poitiers

Order in the court!

They were all gathered in the Visitation prison courtroom in Poitiers. Everyone important, that is. Mayor Sylvain Biron was there, elbow to elbow with the Bishop Aimé Dulaire, Dean Adrien de Fresnay of the university's prestigious Faculté des Lettres, Dr. Pierre Bauché, director of the medical school, and Pastor Jacques Leber. All of Poitiers high society wanted to attend, but since the hall was not that big, some had lost out. Two surgeons had abandoned their operating rooms to come see the trial. The Prefect Paul Ducas and his Subprefect François Tranchant would not have missed it for the world. Letizia de Marcillat and her husband had only to cross the street to get there. They came with their daughter Henriette and son-in-law Martin Launier.

The defendants, Françoise Meunier and her son, looked guilty. Olivier Salneure, the royal assistant public prosecutor, was accusing them of the premeditated murder of Jean Courlivant. It was not this family's first run-in with the law, which was yet another reason to presume them guilty. Françoise Meunier's father had been guillotined for murder. It was the first thing the assistant public prosecutor mentioned, and as he did, the room vibrated with excitement.

After that, despite contradictory statements from forty witnesses, the case seemed cut and dried; the two defendants had to be guilty. Although their minds were already made up, neither the audience nor the jury seemed to want it to end. People listened to the witnesses and commented on each testimony. Poitiers was normally a very boring place, so a jury trial was always an entertaining diversion.

Martin Launier was on the jury. He had just been appointed to teach rhetoric at the Royal Academy in Poitiers and was hoping to become a professor of French literature in the university's literary division, the Faculté des Lettres, for he was an ambitious man. His young wife Henriette was sure everyone in the courtroom was looking at her, or at least that they had seen her. After all, that's why she had come.

For an hour, Olivier Salneure, facing the jury, had been center-stage. He intended to convince the jurors that certain people, much like bloodthirsty animals, thought solely of destruction. The only way to protect society from them was to decapitate them. The prosecutor was preaching to the choir, as they say. For Martin Launier and the other jurors, it was a foregone conclusion that the two filthy, thickheaded individuals in the defendants' box were guilty.

Maître Duplaisset, attorney for the defense, nonetheless tried to do the impossible: to show that there might be some doubt about the culpability of the defendants. Should a man and a woman be sent to the guillotine, to their death, simply because someone else in their family was guillotined?

With an admirable flourish of the voluminous sleeves of his robe, he stated to the jury: "Gentlemen, you are being asked to make a terrible decision. Think carefully, and be wary that one day the voice of reason may arise, but it will be too late. Yes! It is a thousand times better to let a guilty man go free than to condemn the innocent to death!"

It was a beautiful gesture, but no one took it seriously. The jurors had been asking themselves for days how anyone could possibly defend such rabble.

Jacob Lomet, the young Protestant attorney seated next to Maître Duplaisset, was the only one who agreed.

The expected verdict was delivered: "Guilty!"

A shiver of pleasure rippled through the crowd.

❦

Noon, May 6, 1847: The execution

René and his mother Françoise exited the prison. Across the street at 21 Rue de la Visitation, the de Marcillat residence, all of the staff were pressed against the windows. The butler and the maids would not go to Place du Pont-Guillon, where the guillotine was located, but at least they would have seen something. Monsieur and Madame de Marcillat, along with Martin Launier and Henriette, had left quite some time ago to be at the site of the execution.

René was wearing a pair of blue canvas pants and a wrinkled white shirt. He was walking barefoot, slowly, his legs chained together. His head was covered by a thick black cloth that fell down to his chest. His arms hung forward and his wrists were tied together with rope.

His mother, wearing a grey dress, also had her legs chained together. Her dirty white hair, loose, hung down her back. She was also barefoot with her wrists bound. She sobbed continuously and was shaking uncontrollably.

They were accompanied by an escort of eight gendarmes on horseback, two in front, two behind, and two on each side. Following right behind the convicts were the priests: Father Lombard, the prison chaplain, and Father Georget, a young vicar sent by the bishopric to assist Lombard who was carrying a cross that was at least one meter high.

Father Fabrice Lombard had already ministered to some people sentenced to death, but he still wasn't used to it. Last night, he had heard the confession of each of the convicts, one after the other. He was the only one who knew if they deserved to be freed or not. He did not like executions, nor did his assistant, and neither would have chosen to come.

Father Raymond Georget even viewed this task as a punishment imposed on him by the bishop because he always tended to take the easy path. He was tormented by the jeers of the people lining the streets as they passed by. *"À mort!"* they shouted, calling for death. Never in his life had he seen so many hateful faces gathered in one place. He had only one wish: for it to be over. Thinking of Christ on the cross, flanked by two thieves, he couldn't help but observe that Jesus knew how to forgive.

The procession of the condemned took close to twenty minutes to reach Place du Pont-Guillon, where the gallows had been set up at dawn. The convicts felt all of the hate radiating from the people of Poitiers who lined the route. All of the shops along those streets were closed that day out of fear of pillaging by the ever-growing angry mob.

René slowed. Although he could see nothing, he felt that they were approaching the square and his final hour. Beside him, his mother wept unremittingly. He also soon started to cry.

Place du Pont-Guillon was packed with people. Three thousand people, at least, all there to witness the spectacle. The de Marcillat family had arrived at six o'clock in the morning in order to get seats. All four were positioned just behind the barricades set up around the gallows to hold back the crowds. From there, they could see everything. The other jurors were just as close. Everyone was there, including the mayor, the prefect, and the subprefect; the only one missing was Monsignor Dulaire, who hated executions.

Françoise Meunier and her son René arrived. The crowd called for blood: *"À mort! À mort!"*

Father Lombard spoke quietly with the man, while Father Georget talked to his mother. A few words to comfort them.

The executioners had already begun their work. With a large pair of scissors, the executioner from Saintes was chopping off the woman's hair, while the one from Poitiers was cutting the man's hair and removing the collar of his shirt to free his neck.

The two priests held out the crucifix to be kissed.

A gendarme began the slow beating of the drum. One of the executioners pushed the woman forward, but she refused to move. Two gendarmes grabbed her and forced her head into the guillotine. In an instant, the head rolled onto the square. The crowd, delirious, burst into thunderous applause.

It was the man's turn. He also had to be pulled towards the guillotine, resisting and crying out in fear and desperation. The guillotine blade dropped. He was silenced. The two heads rested on the ground, which had been covered with sand that morning to avoid any permanent stains.

People pushed through the barriers to dip their clean handkerchiefs into the blood spurting out from the severed heads. It seems they believed it would bring good luck.

On that day, without distinction between social classes, all of Poitiers was happy.

When the spectacle was over, everyone headed back to their homes. Carriages packed with people formed a continuous double line all the way down Boulevard de la Préfecture to the Porte de Paris gate. People and their horses were starting to tire of waiting. The sun, at its zenith in the sky, blared down, and coachmen struggled to keep control of horses anxiously stomping on the ground and balking in their harnesses.

People started to get out of their carriages to chat with each other on the sidewalks. They talked casually about the morning's events.

The de Marcillat family, in their elegant tan leather carriage, waited patiently for the line to move. In the distance, they could see the rooftop of their mansion shining brilliantly against the deep blue sky. They felt tired but at peace, as if they had just woken up after a long voyage back from the countryside. They were still dizzy from all of the morning's heady emotion.

Letizia de Marcillat wanted to get out, for she adored gossip and would be in her element there on the sidewalk, but it was so hot out. Instead, she smiled and tried to catch the eye of those in the street, gesturing hello to anyone who smiled back at her. Always affable and gregarious, she was a very beautiful brunette who radiated life, and that day, as was quite common, one could discern a mischievous glint in her dark eyes.

Louis de Marcillat, who was typically happy when his wife was happy, nonetheless felt uncomfortably stuffed into his frock coat. From time to time, he would wipe his brow with a handkerchief, exclaiming "That's some heat!" He was rather a tall man, rather blond, rather plump too, with a long mustache that curled up neatly on each end.

The sun was decidedly strong that day, one of those sweltering days Poitiers is known to have. That night, there would be a storm, perhaps even some hail, with hailstones as big as marbles. But for now, they waited, in the stifling heat and on a street without a single tree to provide any shade.

Henriette, the daughter of the de Marcillats, found the sight of all of these coaches brimming with people stacked up in front of them, behind them, and alongside them, to be quite oppressive. So, she and her husband had set off to return home on foot.

She never had her mother's amiable presence, though she held herself well. And she might even be considered pretty, if her face ever expressed anything other than grave seriousness. Everything about her was stiff: her clothes, her hair, her posture... Everyone found her boring, even her husband, though he was grateful for it because it meant she was someone he could count on. She was a dutiful wife who did everything her husband asked of her. Her husband had wanted her to attend the execution, so she did. Now that everyone had seen her, she had only one thought in mind: to go back home. She had grown tired of the crowds.

While her mother loved to socialize, she did not. She was only happy at home or at Saint-Porchaire Church. Nervous, anxious, always expecting the worst, Henriette never thought of what she wanted to do, but rather asked herself what had to be done. She was there to witness the execution because she had to be. Her husband Martin Launier was nothing but proper: she had to be seen. If she hadn't attended, it would have been viewed as an insult to all of high society in Poitiers, and Martin wanted more than anything to make a good impression on them. He was determined, having just applied to become a literature professor at the Faculté des Lettres, and he fully expected to become dean of the college one day. So, he kept an eye on his wife's social reputation to ensure that she reflected well on him. After all, that's why he had married her.

Henriette may not have been an attractive woman, but she was a de Marcillat. Her father had a good job as a stockbroker in the city and descended from one of the oldest noble families in Poitiers. And Henriette's mother was the granddaughter of one of Napoléon's generals. She was a good catch for the son of a humble hairdresser, a young teacher who dreamt of becoming a professor and a dean.

Twenty-two-year-old Henriette Launier walked nervously towards their home. Would this horrid day ever end? At noon, the sight of the two bloody heads had almost made her vomit. Even thinking about it later turned her stomach. Her husband held her arm as they walked, but she had no one to talk to about how disgusted she was by the whole scene. She had to be dignified, as a professor's wife should be.

Walking alongside his wife, Martin felt perfectly content. He had been able to chat with the prefect, the dean of the Faculté des Lettres, and the director of the medical school. It was a day to be remembered. The closer they got to the mansion that belonged to his in-laws, where they also resided, the happier he felt.

When they arrived at 21 Rue de la Visitation, Martin Launier's thoughts turned to the boudoir, and in fact, he could think of nothing else. To be on the jury of one capital execution case would have been exciting enough, but to have been involved in two executions! As he entered the door held open by the butler, Valentin Durieu, he could not stop smiling.

Once in their suite, Martin Launier took it upon himself to undress his wife, enthusiastically pulling up her skirts. For a month afterward, he was full of vim and vigor.

Nine months later, Honoré, their first child, was born.

∾

February 1848

The banquet campaign was fully underway. In every French city, prominent Républicains gathered influential men together around a table and tried to sway them to their view that France should embrace democracy and hold real elections. They talked politics during the whole meal.

Maître Jacob Lomet organized the banquet held in Poitiers at the Hôtel de la Paix in Place d'Armes on February 20. In the time since the Meunier executions, he had enjoyed some manner of success; he had opened his own law firm and was starting to make a name for himself. His political opinions helped him to win new clients.

He was born to be an orator, and he could warm up a room better than anyone.

Since last August, he had crisscrossed the region from one end to the other, hitting all the big cities in Poitou, Charente, and Vendée. There had been fifteen banquets in all like the one in Poitiers. And Jacob Lomet was a true spokesperson for the Républicains. He was able to persuade, inspire, and move his listeners. Though his banquet circuit had started off quietly, it ended triumphantly. The noble families of Poitiers saw him as a dangerous agitator, but among his friends, he was considered an incomparable leader. His wife accompanied him in all of his travels. She was at his side for this last dinner as well.

All this political talk made everyone hungry, and the menu did not disappoint: Provençal soup, filet of sole with crayfish, veal cutlet en papillote, roasted duck with root vegetables, apple tart. All washed down with endless bottles of good Algerian wine.

Lucien Boulaide stood and declared: "We are the heart of this nation." A humble court officer, he succinctly conveyed all of the suffering felt by the *petite bourgeoisie*, the white-collar middle class. This was indeed what drew them all together. Through their work, they were all helping to build the nation, but none had the right to vote. Professionals and merchants were good for getting things done but were denied any real power, as only those who could afford to pay the *cens* property tax could vote.

It was not an accident that, hanging the full length of one whole wall of the restaurant, there was a large banner that read: "Long live universal suffrage!"

Conversations at the banquets would heat up quickly with the help of flowing wine, and with each course, there would be new social commentary. The jeweler Gaboriau spoke next, saying aloud what all were quietly thinking: "Without freedom of the press, we will never truly have the right to vote."

Louis de Reduré, a poor farmer, went even further: "We want to be able to assemble, whenever we want, wherever we want, without needing authorization!"

Someone bellowed a revolutionary call to end nepotism and monopolies on government positions: "Down with multiple appointments!" What good was the Revolution if years later the same people were still holding all of the important government posts?

At the end of the meal, when Jacob Lomet rose to give a final toast, it was to the Republic. His *"Vive la République, vive la France!"* was met with thunderous applause from the sixty-nine attendees. "Long live the Republic," they shouted, "long live France!"

Without a doubt, Jacob Lomet's banquet campaign had been a rousing success.

Nestled into his armchair, Martin Launier was reading the Courrier de la Vienne et des Deux-Sèvres, a newspaper that portrayed events happening in Paris in the darkest possible way. Though in fact it was true, things weren't going well in the capital.

The newspaper laid it all out: Louis-Philippe, king of France since 1830, gave in to mounting public pressure and abdicated the throne, fleeing to England and leaving his grandson, the Comte de Paris, to rule the nation. Louis-Philippe's trusted minister, François Guizot, a complete disgrace, was ousted. The National Guard, infected by Républicains, no longer obeyed Adolphe Thiers, the conservative minister notorious for using force to suppress any budding insurrections during the reign of Louis-Philippe. Thiers had called on the army to remove all of the barricades that had been set up around Paris. An angry mob had gathered, and General Bugeaud had fired into the crowd. There were casualties on both sides. According to the newspaper, the rioters were just a rag-tag group of nobodies who had been wandering around Paris for three days with corpses on their pikes.

Finally, on February 25, the revolutionary government authorized everything the Républicains desired: freedom to assemble, freedom of the press, the abolition of slavery in the colonies, universal suffrage. But to what end? And to top it all off, now factory workers could join the National Guard.

For Martin Launier, the only positive outcome of this mess was that there would be jobs for the unemployed. Idleness was truly the mother of all vices. All this turmoil had surely been caused by unemployment.

"It's another revolution," the journalist added, fearing the worst. Parisian Républicains, who had been denied their banquet assembly, were the root cause of these events. They were inciting violence across the nation to force electoral reform. They were in charge. There was chaos everywhere. With them, there was no concept of respect, no morality.

Martin Launier and the whole de Marcillat family were wondering, like many of this paper's readers, whether they too should flee to England like the king. Would they still be allowed to go to church? Were priests going to be forced to swear allegiance to the Constitution? Should conservatives take up arms to defend their faith? Would this become another Reign of Terror where aristocrats would be executed without pity? It was one thing to know why the protests had started, but who knew where it might end?

Above all, Martin Launier asked himself out loud whether he would be able to keep his teaching position. He was married to a Royalist, and if the Républicains continued to gain power, they might not think twice about firing him. His fears were stoked by the fact that Maître Lomet's name was plastered on every wall in town. Despised by the wealthy *haute bourgeoisie* in Poitiers, in the de Marcillat home, he was incessantly scorned. They called him "the Revolutionary," that's how scared they were of him!

All this news and her husband's fears destabilized Henriette Launier, who was expecting a baby at any moment. Since it was her first pregnancy, she was already worried about the birth, and now with everything that was going on, she was in a panic.

She no longer left her chamber. She had been moved to a quiet room overlooking the garden to try to calm her nerves, and Marie Pinaud, one of the maids, slept in the room with her in a second bed. They had been waiting for the birth for several days. The youngest of the maids was repeatedly sent to get Pierre Bauché, the director of the medical school, as he was the only doctor that Martin Launier would allow at her bedside.

Honoré Launier was born in Poitiers on February 29, 1848. In Paris, the Second Republic had been declared, and the famed poet Lamartine had convinced the public to approve the colors of the new French flag: blue, white, and red.

April 23, 1848

In front of the main entrance to the Hôtel de Ville, Poitiers' city hall, an immense flag banded with blue, white, and red fluttered in the wind. It was perfect weather, and men flocked towards the building to cast their votes. An endless line curled up the stairs to the function hall where the voting urn was located. Women, who did not have the right to vote, waited outside with their children. That day, they were electing a Constituent Assembly to form the new government.

With the fall of the king and all of the recent riots, resources had been funneled out of the country. The incessant workers' protests with their scuffles, like those in March and the beginning of April, made the country look unstable. Unemployment was on the rise, and two hundred thousand people were out of work, lingering in the cafés of Paris and maintaining revolutionary pressure on the government, which was frightening. Many factories had closed due to lack of orders, and the stock market was crumbling. Everyone was unhappy: the workers were hungry, and the middle class was scared.

At the Hôtel de Ville, they had hastily removed the portrait of Louis-Philippe, the beloved king of the *haute bourgeoisie*. In its place, they hung the tricolor flag.

The voting urn, two meters wide and one meter deep, had been made of beautiful varnished pine by local carpenter Justin Larot. The mayor, Sylvain Biron, sat beside it as closely as he could get, shaking hands with everyone right and left.

After morning mass ended, Monsignor Aimé Dulaire and his diocesan vicars, along with the priests of various parishes, had come to vote in unison for the Royalist candidate, and they did not bother to hide it. The word "republic" alone was enough to send shivers up their spines. They did not want a repeat of what happened in 1789. And Aimé Dulaire knew what he was talking about. He was ten years old then, and his brother had been a vicar.

Prefect Paul Ducas and Subprefect François Tranchant had also come to vote together, also for the Royalist candidate, but they did not feel the need to let that be known. The prefect had spent some time thinking about whether he should vote Royalist in order to keep his post, or just take a chance on the Républicains. Either way, he would need to reach out to both sides so as not to compromise himself and be dismissed after the elections, if Maître Lomet and his band of Républicains happened to win.

Poitiers' aristocratic families arrived in early afternoon.

Dr. Pierre Bauché, director of the medical school, and Dean Adrien de Fresnay of the Faculté des Lettres accompanied the de Marcillat and Launier families. Of course, they each brought their household staff with them, but with strict orders to vote for the Royalist candidate. If not, all mayhem might break loose.

The Protestant pastor, Jacques Leber, known for his Républicain leanings, arrived early along with Jacob Lomet, his wife, and their two maids. A large group of

Républicains had also arrived in the morning: the notary Marc Pessere, the court official Lucien Boulaide, the jeweler Félicien Gaboriau, and Louis de Reduré, who had left his farm to come vote.

The first person to vote was a little old man, a former print shop worker who was over eighty years old. Guillaume Budet had been twenty-three in 1789, and he had been waiting for his chance to vote for years. And, finally, he did it. Once he slipped his ballot into the urn, an uncontrollable smile lit up his face. Then, he waited for the rest. He spent the whole night there, watching the ballots being counted, without ever showing the slightest sign of fatigue.

Other workers also came to vote, wearing new caps on their heads. 1789 had not been forgotten.

After each ballot cast and each "Voted!" called out, people broke into small groups and the discussions started. After such an historic act, no one wanted to leave. They all talked about the future. At one point, the room became so jam-packed that the mayor had to call on the gendarmes stationed there to push the crowd out so that other voters could enter.

With the hall partially emptied, groups formed on the stairs and outside in front of the Hôtel de Ville. There, street vendors were selling cheese, bread, ham, or a cup of red wine in exchange for a few coins.

The Royalist candidate was the Marquis de Chauvigny, a well-known man whose private life was often the subject of gossip. He was a close friend of the Launier family.

Maître Lomet, on the heels of his successful banquet campaign, was the candidate for the Républicains. A third candidate, a Socialist named Germain Lerou, was an unknown factory worker who didn't have much hope of winning.

The three tailors who had sewn the new flags for the city hall, proud of their work, came to vote together.

And, of course, the press was there. Reporters peppered the candidates with questions, the tenor of which reflected the political slant of each newspaper. Persons of note were also interviewed, while regular folks, arriving in droves, were of no interest to the journalists. No one imagined that the lower classes might be the ones to tip the scale.

On that sunny day, in front of city hall, hansom cabs dropped off passengers and pulled aside to park for hours on end. People also came to vote on foot, on horseback... It had been a while since there had been such a crowd in Place d'Armes, with so many pretty gowns on display, so many workers standing next to bourgeois gentlemen, so many maids intermingling with countesses.

There was tension in the air as the votes were counted. The mayor's assistant, an accountant, tallied the votes in chalk on a large blackboard.

In this city where the upper classes held so much power, there was an 84% voter turnout. The banquet campaign had worked. The chaos of the final years of Louis-Philippe's reign had led the people to demand change, to seek order. Jacob Lomet, the lawyer, won in a landslide.

The officials elected that day would indeed make changes. Seven months later, on November 4, 1848, it was decided that France would be a Republic with a Constitution, a President elected for four years by popular vote, and an Assembly, also elected, that would have legislative powers.

Paris, June 1848: The makings of a social revolution

Everything changed on June 21, when a decree ordered that the National Workshops be closed, that all unemployed men aged eighteen to twenty-five be enrolled in the military, and that the others return to their villages. The workshops had been established to provide employment and a minimal source of income for those who had come to Paris seeking a way out of poverty. And now the government was turning them away.

The response was violent. The June Days insurrection of 1848 would bring fire and blood back to the streets of Paris.

"Bread and work," that's all the insurgents were asking for. But they didn't get it. The only response was military force. Barricades were set up throughout the city. Weapons were discharged on both sides. The arch-bishop of Paris, Monsignor Affre, had tried to intervene and was killed. The results were staggering: six thousand dead. The national guard had been decimated, and the army had lost fifteen hundred men.

Cavaignac, the Minister of War, succeeded in stomping down the insurrection. He arrested twenty-five thousand people and deported four thousand, including the son of one of the maids in the Lomet household, Jean Loyseau. He had gone to Paris to find work, and ended up being sent to Algeria in chains.

The people of Poitiers followed the events in Paris through the newspapers. Fear rose once again amongst the Royalists. Indeed, 1789 was not that long ago. Those fears dissipated as order was restored and summer approached.

The Launiers already had a son. Now Martin Launier wanted a daughter. It was part of his career plan. A respectable family must have a son—for sure—and a daughter. It had to be done. A daughter could be married to someone influential. A well-positioned son-in-law was always a plus...

This was Martin Launier's thinking early on in his teaching career. Son of a modest hairdresser, he had to go above and beyond if he wanted to succeed.

He sensed his wife's reticence. Some days, she even spoke to him about how wonderful it was to see happy families with only one child. Henriette Launier argued that with an only child, the family's estate would not be diluted, as it would all fall to one heir. One son was sufficient.

It was not that she feared another childbirth. No, certainly not. She had suffered some, but no more than others. The problem was that she had gotten heavier since her pregnancy, and she obsessed about her weight. She was a woman who took great pride in her looks and felt that carrying a baby for nine months made a woman look ugly. To keep her figure, she made a million excuses so that it would not happen to her again.

Truth be told, she didn't really enjoy having sexual relations with her husband either. She wished he could be satisfied with her presence alone.

Martin Launier was the opposite. When Sunday arrived in this glorious month of June, he brought his wife down to the Clain River for a romantic stroll. After nearly a full day of attempts to seduce her, he finally convinced his wife that her beauty couldn't be altered, and there in the Saint-Benoît forest, on a bed of oak leaves, the air perfumed with the scent of honeysuckle, they conceived a daughter.

March 9, 1849

The bells rang out. Blanche Launier, daughter of Martin and Henriette Launier, granddaughter of the de Marcillats, was baptized. Eighteen carriages adorned with flowers waited outside in front of the cathedral. Blanche was entering the Christian world in style.

She had been baptized by the bishop. Little Blanche, just eight days old, accepted the sacrament without a tear. Monsignor Dulaire anointed her with the holy chrism, and there was not a peep out of her. She was smiling. Though she didn't know it, she was joyously renouncing Satan and all of his works and surrendering herself to God to become a child of the Church.

The Marquis de Chauvigny, her godfather, held her in his arms at the baptismal font. He was around forty years old, with curly grey hair and a long mustache. His family had always been very close to the de Marcillat family. There were even some marriages linking the two bloodlines. Blanche's godmother, on the other hand, was not related to her at all. She was the wife of the principal at the Royal Academy where her father taught, which was reason enough for her to be chosen as godmother.

Neither godparent had been consulted when it came to choosing the baby's name. It was Henriette Launier alone who had picked out her full name: Blanche Marie-Antoinette Letizia. "Blanche" was chosen for the medieval French queen, Blanche de Castille, and also because the name symbolized purity. "Marie-Antoinette" was in honor of the former queen, and "Letizia," the name of Napoléon's mother, was also meant to please her own mother, Letizia de Marcillat, who was an ardent Bonapartist. Henriette believed these names would bring good luck to the family.

Henriette insisted that Blanche be dressed in a blue and white gown, reminiscent of the Virgin Mary. She dedicated the child to Mary. The baptismal gown, trimmed with Calais lace, was over a meter long. It was clear that this was meant to be a stunning baptism.

As the bells echoed throughout all of Poitiers and the Launiers passed out sugar-coated almonds to guests in front of Saint-Pierre Cathedral, the proud parents felt their hearts swell with joy.

The horse-drawn carriages adorned with flowers and filled with guests began to parade down the street, and not even the dry cold of early March could dampen their spirits.

Paul Ducas, the local prefect, had lent a hand. He had placed four gendarmes in the street the night before the baptism to ensure that no other carriages parked along Rue de la Visitation that morning.

Good fortune seemed to grace the beautiful mahogany cradle of Blanche Marie-Antoinette Letizia Launier.

II

July 1, 1851

Two and a half years had passed since Louis Napoléon Bonaparte, the son of Napoléon's brother Louis Bonaparte, had been elected President of the Republic by overwhelming majority in a general election held on December 10, 1848. During those years the Prince-President had traveled throughout the country, going from one official ceremony to another, working his charm on the people of France and determined to become Napoléon III.

When he arrived in Poitiers on the first of July to inaugurate the new train station, he came aboard the first train to ever make the trip from Paris to Poitiers. People had come from all over the region to welcome him. He traveled in the lead car, which was as shiny and new as the whole locomotive. Blue, white, and red ribbons wafted in the summer wind.

The Prince-President enjoyed pageantry, so as soon as the train reached the city limit at the Porte de Paris and started to slow down as it wound towards the station, he opened the car door and stepped out onto the running board. All smiles, he waved to the crowds. He was so good at it that when the first onlookers standing on the footbridge of the new station saw him, they shouted "Long live the Emperor!": *"Vive l'Empereur!"*

That day, Louis Napoléon Bonaparte was a happy prince.

He was a man who knew how to surround himself with allies, like the Duc de Morny, the military leader Saint-Arnaud, and the Duc de Persigny. In Poitiers, he had one unconditional supporter: Letizia de Marcillat, a descendant of one of Napoléon's generals. It was due to her initiative that he had come to Poitiers, and she had organized the entire visit.

She had prepared a grandiose welcome, worthy of the future emperor she knew he would become. When he stepped off the train, she was the one to meet him. And Letizia de Marcillat gave herself permission to greet him with open arms. The Prince-President, who was a simple, very private man, was quite moved by this gesture.

The colorful crowd dressed in their Sunday best repeatedly shouted with great enthusiasm: *"Vive l'Empereur!"* On Letizia de Marcillat's request, the orchestra played the Imperial March. One might have thought this scene to have occurred a year later, after Louis Napoléon had actually become the new Emperor of France. The people of Poitiers gave him a hero's welcome, lining the streets from the train station to the Hôtel de Ville and waving bouquets of flowers. From balconies, people threw rose petals at the cortege. It was a celebration.

Martin Launier was luckier than most. His mother-in-law never left the side of her Prince-President. She had pulled out all the stops so that this day would be unforgettable. With the help of the prefect, Paul Ducas, she had held meetings, negotiated, fretted and organized for days, and now that he was at her side, she spoke to him as if they were old friends. The granddaughter of an imperial general, she played her part well. Martin Launier was seated in the front row. He also had a chance to talk to the Prince-President.

Louis Napoléon felt quite at home. All of Poitiers had come to see him, from humble workers to wealthy notables, some because he was the nephew of Napoléon, others because he was President of the Republic, and others still, the bourgeoisie in particular, because business had been good since he had taken office. There were so many new construction projects: avenues, railroads, ships. The prince never stopped attending ribbon-cutting ceremonies, and France was transforming itself into a modern nation where commerce was finally thriving.

Letizia de Marcillat was proud to welcome her Prince-President, but she also had a personal agenda.

She wanted a prestigious post for her son-in-law. Since Martin Launier was a teacher, she had decided that he should become the private tutor to Louis Napoléon's son. For the moment, the Prince-President was still single, but there were whispers of an impending marriage. So, it was the right time to bring it up in conversation.

The Prince-President had every reason to be satisfied with Letizia de Marcillat. She had done good work, and since he was a man who knew how to repay his friends, he thought it proper to thank her in a way that befitted such a beautiful woman. She had spoken to him, between petits fours, about her son-in-law, whom she had introduced, and who was teaching at the Royal Academy.

During the return trip to Paris that warm summer evening, with *"Vive l'Empereur!"* ringing in his ears, the Prince-President decided that he should absolutely hire Letizia de Marcillat's son-in-law as a private tutor one day.

～

January 1, 1858

From Montbernage to Saint-Martin-L'Ars, Poitiers was covered in snow. City workers were shoveling snow from the paved roads as best they could, while fat snowflakes continued to fall, slowly, heavily, blanketing the ground. It had been snowing for a week already, and all indications were that it would continue like this for some time. It was so cold that some water wells had frozen solid. Over by the Saint-Cyprien bridge, the river was frozen all the way up to the courtyard of the Dominicans. It was one of the worst winters in years. The only way to reach the train station was to trudge through snow that was at least thirty centimeters deep!

Inside the station, warmly dressed and surrounded by their luggage, Martin and Henriette Launier waited for the train to Paris. They had purchased their tickets a while ago and their minds were already traveling down the rails. On December 2, 1852, the Prince-President had been proclaimed Emperor Napoléon III, and shortly thereafter, on January 30, 1853, he had married Marie-Eugénie de Montijo de Guzman, Countess of Teba. She was the daughter of a Spanish nobleman. They had a son together, and Martin Launier was called to the imperial court to serve as his tutor. He brought with him his wife, Henriette, and their son, Honoré.

At the request of her de Marcillat grandparents, Blanche would stay in Poitiers. "You'll come visit us. We will come see you. And your grandmother and grandfather are so kind, you'll be fine with them," said Henriette to her daughter, hoping to finish up the goodbyes quickly. Blanche, just nine years old, sobbed and clung to her mother's legs.

When Henriette Launier heard the train whistle blow and saw the locomotive pull into the station, she felt relieved. Blanche, meanwhile, was inconsolable. She had never been away from her mother, and this separation felt insurmountable for the child. Her mother pushed her aside, giving her a quick kiss on the forehead.

Finally, the train was leaving with all of its passengers. Blanche remained behind with her grief, moaning pitifully and calling out for her mother: *"Maman! Maman!"*

Her grandparents, sad to see her suffering so, brought her back to the house. For three days, she cried without respite. Although her *grand-maman* and *grand-papa* tried everything they could think of to get her mind off of the departure, nothing would distract her. Pretty jewels, beautiful outfits, adorable dolls, nothing worked. Even the turtledoves her grandfather bought her did not seem to please her. They had hired local carpenter Justin Larot to build a magnificent cage to house the birds in the garden.

The little girl wasn't sleeping, was barely eating, and tended to throw up what little she managed to swallow.

On the fourth day, the tears dried up. She stopped crying. Because of this traumatic and profoundly sad event, for fifteen years from that time, she never shed another tear, no matter what happened. She didn't cry again until the death of her *grand-maman*, who by then had fully replaced her mother.

～

Paris, January 14, 1858

The opera house was packed. Everyone was waiting for the Emperor. The opera *Orphée aux enfers* was playing that night. The beautiful Hortense Schneider, one of Jacques Offenbach's favorite singers who had captivated Napoléon III, was set to mesmerize all of Paris once again. The tenor, Clapelle, was warming up in the dressing room. Billionaires, princes, people from all over the world had come to admire the prestige and pageantry of Paris.

The Emperor had not yet arrived. All were waiting.

Then, the imperial coaches pulled up in front of the Opéra, with the Emperor and Empress, accompanied by General Roguet, in the first carriage. Just behind them was the carriage with Martin Launier and his wife; beside Henriette was the indefatigable Minister of Commerce, Rouher, famous for collaborating with Haussmann on his plans to redesign and beautify the capital. He was also the one who instigated the draining of swamps throughout France and adorned the country with its network of railways.

Luckily, that night, little Honoré Launier had stayed home in bed.

The horses had just stopped when, all of a sudden, there was a horrific explosion, followed by another and another! Frightened horses reared and neighed in terror. Some carriages were toppled on their sides. The Launiers' flipped over backward, and one of the horses was killed. The horses pulling the imperial coach were seriously wounded.

The Emperor's carriage was hit by eighty pieces of shrapnel. It was a miracle to see the Emperor climb out of the coach, followed by the Empress who, though covered in blood, was alive. General Roguet had been hit in the head, and it was his blood that stained the gown of the Empress.

Some onlookers were also hurt, along with people in the other carriages. There were wounded people everywhere. Bodies were quickly transported to the Hôtel-Dieu hospital. In the end, eight people were killed in the attack and more than 150 injured!

The guards in charge of security for the imperial cortege had also lost some men, but they were able to catch the bombers. They were Italian terrorists: Felice Orsini, a forty-year-old man, was the leader, working with three henchmen, young Italian republicans named Pieri, Gomez, and Rudio.

When the attack occurred, everyone feared for their lives, and the women could not stop trembling... Henriette Launier, who had fainted, had to be transported on a stretcher in one of the carriages that still had its wheels.

Obviously, the performance at the Opéra was canceled, as no one felt like singing. Everyone who had been in the imperial cortege scattered on the sidewalks, flocked to the carriages that were still operational, and headed for the Tuileries.

The Second Empire had narrowly escaped destruction.

〜

March 1858

The Tuileries palace had never witnessed a court as sumptuous as the court of Napoléon III. Among all of the royal courts in Europe, France's stood out for its pomp and splendor. Foreign leaders flocked to see Paris and left feeling in awe. Paris was considered the fashion capital of the world, and it was true. The most beautiful gowns were designed and worn there.

At official events, all eyes were on Empress Marie-Eugénie. Napoléon III could not have hoped for a better ambassador. She was beautiful, radiant even, and dazzled the guests at every ball and reception she organized. Every prince worthy of his title endeavored to attend at least one of her events.

Women wore magnificent jewels that sparkled in contrast to the black suits of the princes on their arms. They spent entire evenings waltzing to the music of Strauss. It was sheer bliss! The court of Napoléon III, it must be noted, was far more brilliant than that of his uncle.

But since the attack that almost took the lives of the Emperor and Empress, things had settled down. People were still getting over the shock of all of the blood and cries of terror. Orsini and Pieri had been judged and condemned to death. Both died on the scaffold shouting nationalist support for Italy and France: *"Vive l'Italie! Vive la France!"* Knowing that they were dead comforted some in the Emperor's court. A new national security policy voted into law by the government helped to reassure the French people.

Orsini and Pieri were Italian republicans. The French Républicains were therefore seen as their accomplices. A whiff of witch hunt lingered in the air. The entire court, traumatized by the event, deduced that every Républicain must, on some level, be a criminal. The Launiers led the pack in this line of thinking.

The fact that Jules Favre, a Républicain, was the lawyer for the defense in the trial of the terrorists only furthered this belief. The police began to raid places where Républicains gathered, and some were arrested and deported to Algeria.

Since the attack, the Empress Marie-Eugénie and all of the ladies of the court had lost interest in going out. One night at the palace, while the Empress sat alone playing solitaire, Henriette Launier engaged in a game of checkers with the Duchess of Artencour.

Martin Launier was there as well, waiting for Napoléon III to retire to his study so that he could do the same. He was suddenly inspired to work on his thesis. Believing the capital to be too dangerous, he and his wife both desperately wanted to return to Poitiers.

The Emperor was speaking in a low voice to the Maréchal Vaillant, while the Maréchal de Saint-Arnaud, a great horseman, and the Maréchal Magnan, a great hunter, were engaged in a game of chess nearby.

It was just before nine o'clock when the Emperor decided to retire, and Martin Launier, followed by his wife, quickly did so as well.

∽

June 27, 1861

The day had come for Blanche's First Communion ceremony in the church. Her parents had returned to Poitiers, after three years away, in order to attend.

The children lined up in the church, girls to the left and boys to the right, the smallest in front and the tallest in the back. With large candles in their hands, they proceeded slowly towards the altar. Monsignor Aimé Dulaire's eyes welled with joy.

Blanche had just turned twelve, but looked like she was sixteen. She was in the back with the older children and was the tallest of them all.

Martin and Henriette Launier, who never would have recognized her had she come alone to meet them at the train station, looked on with pride at their beautiful young girl. The day was slipping by quickly, and they planned to return to Paris by train that night. Did they even have time to get to know Blanche, who had changed so much?

Blanche had seemed excited to see them again. It was a day to celebrate, and everyone was together. That was the one thing she most desired. She would have been hurt if they had made some excuse not to come, as they had for each of her birthdays and other holidays. On regular days, she didn't miss her parents at all. Over the years, she had learned not to. Anyway, for quite some time, her grandmother de Marcillat had taken on the role of her mother, and her grandfather that of her father. As for her brother, he had changed so much that she barely knew him.

Blanche was beautiful. Tall and slender, she had thick black hair that fell all the way down her back. Her mother hated it; she would have preferred to see her daughter's hair in braids. Loose hair like that was an unpardonable sign of sloppiness. But by the time she had realized it, the ceremony was about to begin, so she had to let it go. Henriette Launier did not recognize her daughter and felt completely disconnected from her.

Madame Launier sat up straight as a pin between her husband and her father, thinking that Blanche, in her white veil, looked more like a bride than a child at a First Communion ceremony. Her dress was too fitted, too lavishly embellished, and not completely white due to the pink roses embroidered on it. It must have been her own mother's idea. Her daughter should have worn a simple white tunic, stiff and straight. Who was responsible for this outfit, mother or daughter? Both of them, surely. Henriette had fulfilled her obligation by attending that day, but at times wondered if she should have. She couldn't help but feel a tiny pinch of jealousy to think that her mother had replaced her in her daughter's eyes.

Her time at the imperial court had made her haughty. Here, people nodded hello to her, and she responded in kind but was unable to put names to the faces. Old acquaintances, perhaps, or friends of her parents... She couldn't stop herself from thinking that her daughter had become the wrong type of girl. Kneeling in the church pew, she resolved not to comment on it that day, so as not to spoil the celebration, but she would write to her mother next week to express her opinions and provide guidance concerning Blanche's upbringing.

She suppressed her bad mood, although it was difficult, and offered an impassive face to the world despite her discontent. All day long, she made sure not to raise her voice and to seem amiable, even though she felt the same pang in her stomach that she used to feel any time someone contradicted her. After the ceremony, she couldn't help herself and pulled her daughter aside. She talked to her about principles and the importance of remaining virtuous, speeches that Blanche found extremely boring. She ended with a warning: life is full of dangers, so you need to be cautious. The whole time she was lecturing her daughter, she held her head up and spoke calmly, without raising her voice, in a way that communicated distance and superiority.

Blanche listened to all this with an air of polite indifference, which her mother perceived. Once again, Henriette Launier was jealous of her own mother who was raising Blanche her way and keeping her to herself.

The meal itself was wonderful. The table was set beautifully and the guests seated around it were having a splendid time. Monsignor Dulaire was at the party, along with the prefect and several other notable people. But Henriette Launier was never able to relax. She did not smile, not even once, the entire evening. She felt superfluous, and that feeling did not go away.

At the end of the day, when she boarded the train for Paris with her son and her husband, she had a terrible migraine that she was unable to shake for days to come.

∿

1864

Bursting out in laughter, Blanche was running around the dining room table, being chased by Céline Thébaud who was demanding the return of her cooking pot.

"Give that back to me, you little rascal, or there will be no pie for you!" the cook shouted.

Letizia de Marcillat, who had heard the ruckus, had come running to find out what was going on, but instead of scolding, a smile spread across her face. She liked to see her granddaughter so happy and full of life. The girl's childhood antics made her laugh, and although she instructed her to return the pot, deep inside she was thinking that Blanche was just adorable.

"Sweetheart, give that cooking pot back or we will have nothing to eat today."

Her grandmother's voice stopped her in her tracks, and even though she wasn't afraid of her, she obeyed. She loved her grandmother, so she gave the pot back to the cook, who returned to the kitchen red-faced from running around the table.

"I'm bored, *grand-maman*," Blanche said.

Letizia de Marcillat affectionately stroked the girl's forehead: "This afternoon, I'll bring you with me to see a trial."

Letizia de Marcillat simply adored court trials. Whether it was a jury trial or a sentencing in the correctional court, she never missed a single one. One hour in the courthouse was all it took for her to forget all her other worries. Blanche was so much like her grandmother, and they got along so well, that it was a good bet that Blanche would also enjoy them.

They did resemble each other quite a bit. Blanche, like her grandmother, was thin and fit. She had the same big black eyes and the same smooth white skin.

Letizia de Marcillat did not look like a sixty-one-year-old. Thanks to a product her daughter would send her from Paris, she had not even one white hair. Beautifully coquettish, elegant in looks and style, she made Blanche quite proud to be seen with her. They shared many of the same likes and dislikes, and they both loved to go out and socialize. They always accepted invitations and never missed a party or a dinner.

The courthouse was the only place that Letizia de Marcillat hadn't yet brought her granddaughter. Blanche was fifteen and had finished school; now was the time. So, a little before one o'clock in the afternoon, the pair headed off to the Palais de Justice, which was just across the street. The trial they attended was a correctional matter of little interest to most regular folks. The attorney, Gilles Lomet, was from the Jacob Lomet law firm; he was Jacob's son. Recently admitted to the bar, the young Protestant lawyer was arguing his first case in court.

He was slender and handsome and looked good in his crisp new robe. Just twenty-six years old, his voice projected confidently throughout the courtroom, one might go so far as to say it thundered, even though the case he was arguing, about a property line dispute between two stubborn neighbors, did not require such intensity. He had sparkling grey-blue eyes, blonde well-coiffed hair, a neatly groomed mustache, everything required to make a woman take note, and plenty did. Once she laid eyes on him, Blanche saw nothing else. Even Letizia de Marcillat was enchanted by him. As they were leaving the courthouse, Letizia took it upon herself to ask the bailiff the name of this handsome new lawyer.

Happy Days

Blanche had become a ravishing young woman whose giggles and laughter were part of everyday life in the de Marcillat household, characterizing many a conversation. Even though neither her parents nor her brother had come back to Poitiers since her First Communion, her life was there, in Poitiers, and she was happy.

Her day began at nine o'clock in the morning. She slept very well at night and would wake up full of energy. First on her agenda was to go downstairs to have breakfast with her grandparents. Émilie Frasié, the maid, would bring her a big bowl of hot chocolate with fresh bread still warm from the oven and little pots of butter and jam. She was always starving in the morning and happily gobbled it all up.

After breakfast on weekdays, Mademoiselle Ursule Manin, her piano teacher, would come to the house. In the salon, she learned to play piano and to sing. For several hours, the whole house was full of music and song.

Next, Blanche would go outside to care for her turtledoves. The birdcage was in the garden near the well. Many broods had hatched since her grandfather had gifted her the birds on the day her parents had left for Paris. She had been only nine years old... Now, she had a dozen turtledoves that she fed three times a day. Often, in the evenings, she would come back out again to check on them and admire their beautiful feathers. Balanced on their perches, the birds would coo from dawn to dusk. When the weather was warm, Blanche liked to go to bed with the window open so she could hear them as she fell asleep and as soon as she woke up.

At lunchtime, in the de Marcillat home, there were almost always invited guests. Both Louis de Marcillat and his wife enjoyed good company, and meals would last for hours. Letizia de Marcillat used to send the invitations, and she had an address book full of interesting and important people. Meals were never boring. The de Marcillats also properly received guests for lunch on

Sundays. On those days, they would stay at the table until at least four o'clock.

After meals, there would be musical entertainment, as Blanche's grandparents loved to hear her play piano and have their guests hear her too. Blanche always accepted graciously. She loved Schubert and enjoyed playing as much as she enjoyed entertaining their guests. Why learn the piano, she often mused, if no one is there to listen to you play? She also particularly enjoyed when people applauded at the end of a piece she played.

During the week, in the afternoons after the guests left, Louis de Marcillat used to go out for a walk in the city or on his land—he owned several farms—while Letizia and Blanche got dressed for their outing to the Palais de Justice.

From 1864, the year she attended her first trial, to 1871, Blanche never missed a single case in court. Letizia had indeed passed on her passion to her granddaughter. Thus, at least once a week and sometimes more, Blanche was able to see and hear Gilles Lomet, the young man who had become the focus of her daydreams.

After a trial, the two women would go for a walk in Blossac Park. There, when it was nice out, they would see all the prominent bourgeois families in Poitiers. People would chat, children would play ball or cricket, invitations were extended.

On Saturdays, they took walks in the city. They would go to the market or go window-shopping in streets lined with fancy boutiques. Letizia de Marcillat wanted Blanche to be the most beautiful girl in any room. She spared no expense purchasing parasols, hats, dresses, shoes, sunbonnets. Money was no object. She was just happy to provide the best for her granddaughter.

On Sunday mornings, Blanche, her grandparents, and all of the household staff would go to church. The family would attend the high mass at the cathedral, where they had a designated pew. The staff would go to Saint-Porchaire Church for the six o'clock mass.

In the afternoons, Blanche and her grandmother would often be invited to an acquaintance's home. Grandfather de Marcillat preferred to go hunting or fishing whenever he could. He preferred that to socializing, allowing his wife to take the lead in that area.

In the summer, however, they would all take the train together to La Rochelle for a swim in the sea. They would leave early in the morning, usually accompanied by one maid, Émilie Frasié. They would arrive at eleven o'clock and go straight to services. At noon, they would go to a restaurant for fresh oysters. Then, they would head to the beach, where grandfather would rent a cabana. The day would be magical, and Blanche would play it over and over in her mind all week long. She would swim, run on the beach, play ball with other young women from Poitiers, take walks on the pier.

The four of them would return on the last train back to Poitiers, arriving at Rue de la Visitation around midnight. Each would go to their quarters, quickly clean up, and drop into a deep sleep of contentment.

Louis de Marcillat could honestly say to his Parisian daughter, in his weekly letter to her, that Blanche was really quite happy with them.

∽

August 25, 1868

The new prefecture had just been completed, and it was time for an official event to unveil the space to the public. Durand, the architect hired to do the construction project, had begun his work in 1864. It took four years to build the Empire-style building of red brick and white stone. Actually, the building plans had been drawn up by the famous Baron Haussmann when he was secretary of the prefecture in 1831. Some time had passed between the planning and construction phases.

For years, the people of Poitiers would pass in front of the work zone wondering when this project would be completed. Now, it was complete, and the eagles that adorned it indicated clearly that it was built in honor of Napoléon III.

Whether Républicain or Bonapartist, all agreed that it was a beautiful building. But what would become of the old prefecture, which was quite small and lacked grandeur? No one knew.

Blanche was now nineteen. And the next evening, she would attend her first ball.

Letizia de Marcillat had purchased a floor-length blue organdy dress that Blanche would wear to the ball, her hair done up with ribbons and topped off by a sapphire tiara. It was the tiara she had worn the day that she first met Louis. To enhance the look, she had Blanche try on some of her jewelry. They both agreed on a gold necklace with a large pearl. It was a gem that would make her stand out, a gem for a young woman. Blanche tried it on over and over again.

Of course, her grandparents would accompany her to the ball, and they hoped to be as stylish as their granddaughter. Letizia had bought herself a lilac dress for the occasion and had purchased a fashionable black suit for her husband.

Letizia had not been out dancing for quite some time, so she decided to stay in and rest up the day before. This meant that Blanche would go to the courthouse alone that day. And it was her lucky day, as Gilles Lomet was arguing the case on the docket.

After the trial, instead of the usual nod she would give as she caught his eye, she mustered up her courage, walked straight over to him, and quickly said: "I'm going to the ball at the prefecture tomorrow!" It was brief, but the message was received. Attorney Gilles Lomet, who was about thirty-one years old, had long been wondering how to approach this young woman he had seen so often in the courtroom. That night, he asked his mother for advice about what to wear to the ball.

On August 25, when he entered the hall at the prefecture where all of Poitiers was gathered under shiny new chandeliers, he scanned the room looking for the young woman whose name he did not know, even though he had locked eyes with her for years at the courthouse. Once he found her, he did not let her out of his sight. When the band launched into the first waltz, he marched over to Louis de Marcillat, whom he believed to be the girl's father, to ask permission to dance with her.

Blanche danced with Gilles Lomet all night long. Only Letizia de Marcillat knew who he was and that he was a Républicain. She made a point not to tell her husband. It wasn't yet time. Her granddaughter was radiant and happy, and that's all that mattered. Her husband was also content, as he found the young man to be quite distinguished.

Letizia and Louis also danced every waltz the orchestra played.

Before going to the prefecture ball, Blanche had already fallen for Gilles, but ever since the ball, she was truly in love. Not a day would go by that she wouldn't see him. The young lawyer was equally smitten. He confided this to his mother, who immediately invited the girl to their home. Gilles lived on one floor of his parents' house, and now, on Sunday afternoons, Blanche would come to visit and enjoy a piece of cake and conversation with Madame Lomet.

Blanche, who hid nothing from her grandmother, told her every detail. Sitting on a bench in Blossac Park, they had a long conversation. Letizia de Marcillat listened with a smile in her heart as she heard Blanche describe everything she had already surmised. She explained to Blanche that marriages could be complicated. Her own parents had wanted her to marry someone other than Louis. She had to convince them. In the end, she succeeded, but Blanche would need to be patient too, she cautioned.

She reminded Blanche that her parents were fiercely opposed to all Républicains and that Gilles' father was a well-known Républicain, and in fact the entire Lomet family was composed of Républicains. She also noted that Blanche's father, though in Paris, was the private tutor of the Emperor's son, all comments that Blanche found to be ridiculous. Letizia told her granddaughter that it was okay to fall in love, advising her to love but also to be good and to take her time. Before she even thought of telling her parents, she should let the relationship grow, take time to be sure of her feelings for him. Also, her grandmother would need time to figure out how to break this news to her parents, for she was sure it would not go well.

Letizia de Marcillat knew her daughter Henriette quite well, and knew she was stubborn. Once she made a decision, she never turned back. She hated the Républicains, almost on a visceral level. As for her son-in-law, the idea of having his daughter marry a Républicain would be insulting. It was not going to be easy. Not at all. Blanche, sitting with her head leaning on her grandmother's shoulder, could think of nothing other than Gilles. Letizia would have to find a way to help them.

That night, Letizia de Marcillat spoke with her husband. Louis, who worked at the stock exchange, was a practical man who had no use for politics. Only one thing mattered to him: the strength of one's financial portfolio. Nothing else was really important.

Letizia waited for her husband to join her in their suite.

"My dear, our Blanche is in love."

"I've noticed this as well. What is the young man's name?"

"You know who I'm talking about?"

"The young man she danced with all night at the pre-fecture ball."

"Exactly! What did you think of him?"

"What does he do for a living?"

"He's a lawyer."

"A good one, I hope?"

"Yes, quite good and with a promising career ahead of him."

"Well, what's his name?"

"His name is Gilles Lomet."

"The son of Jacob Lomet? Really!"

"Precisely, the son of the Républicain deputy."

"Letizia, don't bring politics into everything. His father is the best lawyer in the city. I've sent him many clients."

"He is quite well respected. And Gilles is an only child."

"How old is he?"

"Thirty."

"At that age, you know what you want. We should see that they marry, my dear, and soon."

"I agree, but our daughter and her husband..."

"So what? Because he's a Républicain? Big deal. He is rich and will continue to be so, that's what matters. With him, our Blanche will want for nothing."

"Henriette despises Républicains, especially ever since the attack on the Emperor."

"Try to make her see reason for once. This Gilles Lomet is the best catch in Poitiers."

"It's not just Henriette. Martin is the Emperor's son's tutor."

"When it comes to choosing a son-in-law, you ask how much money he has, not what he thinks. If we had wanted Henriette to marry for our beliefs, we would have married her to a baron. I will remind her that we decided on a teacher at the Royal Academy because he was more stable."

"We should wait to speak with them, you know how stubborn the two of them are."

"As you wish, but take care of it before this opportunity slips away."

III

July 19, 1870

The war of 1870 between France and Prussia struck France like lightning on a summer night. With only slight provocation, Napoléon III's Prime Minister Émile Ollivier, "with a light heart," declared war on Prussia on July 19. The Prussian Kaiser, Wilhelm I, had simply refused to receive the Ambassador of France, and his Prime Minister, Otto von Bismarck, had bragged about it in the infamous Ems dispatch: "His Majesty refused the ambassador and told him through his aide-de-camp that he had nothing more to say to him."

The wounded pride of the French leaders would bring about the end of the empire.

According to the generals, this should have been a very short and quick war. Indeed, it was, as it only lasted a month and a half, but it was a costly one. They said France was prepared for it. Victory would be swift. History tells a different tale.

Maréchal Patrice de MacMahon, who commanded 63,000 soldiers, was charged with defending Alsace. Maréchal François-Achille Bazaine, with 140,000 men, had the nearby Lorraine region. The French weakness was artillery, at which the Prussians excelled.

First, there was a victory: at Saarbrücken, on August 2. Then, things took a turn for the worse, and one defeat followed another. On August 4, General Douay pulled back, while MacMahon regrouped in Frœschwiller. But on the sixth of August, the Prussian artillery immobilized the French. At Morsbronn, despite the charge of the Reichshoffen cuirassiers, the French were defeated. After incessant gunfire and hand-to-hand combat, the Prussians concentrated their firepower on Frœschwiller and took it. MacMahon decided to turn back towards Saverne rather than join the forces in Lorraine. This was his downfall. On the other front, Maréchal Bazaine, who had been defeated at Forbach, had retreated to Metz. They were quickly surrounded and remained on the defensive.

Determined to regain the offensive position, MacMahon called his troops together to the camp at Chalons, where the Emperor and his forces joined them. But, at Beaumont, on August 30, the troops led by Général de Failly were overpowered, forcing MacMahon to retreat to Sedan. The Prussians trapped him there, and on September 2, the French surrendered. The

Prussians took 83,000 prisoners, including Napoléon III himself.

As soon as the news reached Paris, the Républicains led a crowd of people to the Palais Bourbon, the meeting place of the National Assembly. Led by Républicain Léon Gambetta, they declared an end to the empire and proclaimed a new republic. Quickly, a National Defense government was formed. It was on September 4, 1870 at the Hôtel de Ville in Paris. Général Louis-Jules Trochu became head of the National Defense government and de facto head of state. Jules Favre became Minister of Foreign Affairs and Gambetta took over as Minister of the Interior.

During this time, the Prussian army was preparing to descend on Paris...

The day the Third Republic was declared, supporters of the empire at the Tuileries palace were swept up into a full panic. A few of the faithful surrounded the Empress, trying to comfort her, while others fled. The Launiers were among the latter. They packed their bags with record speed and did not say goodbye to the Empress. They took the first coach available to the Gare d'Orléans and hopped on the next train to Poitiers.

The Prussian siege of Paris began on September 19. On October 2, Gambetta fled the besieged capital in a hot air balloon, hoping to organize the next phase of the war from the countryside.

∽

Poitiers, February 1871

Although Blanche's parents were back, she hadn't yet spoken to them about her love for Gilles Lomet. It didn't seem to be the right moment. The whole house was filled with such agitation; it was not the time to share her secret. In any case, her parents had more important things to do than to listen to her.

They were living in the house, but they weren't really there. Her father was fixated on finding a teaching appointment, and both parents were gearing up for the next election when the country would finally decide: France would either be a constitutional monarchy or it would be a republic. The French would be electing deputies for the Constituent Assembly. Trochu's National Defense government was able to get a three-week armistice in exchange for surrendering Paris, in order to allow for the election of the new National Assembly and peace negotiations.

Once again, to Blanche's great disappointment, Poitiers would be divided between Républicains, led by Gilles' father Jacob Lomet, and Royalists, led by Blanche's godfather the Marquis de Chauvigny. Blanche's parents clung to the Marquis. Temporarily without employment, Martin Launier had become his right-hand man in the electoral campaign that clearly was not going to be an easy win.

Henriette Launier was her husband's shadow, following him everywhere. She was, however, a quite efficient helper and gave her opinion about everything, down to the layout of the campaign posters. She found it all very exciting. In the Marquis de Chauvigny's head-quarters, a room in his château, as in the living room of 21 Rue de la Visitation, the only topic of conversation was how to bury the Républicains and their leader Jacob Lomet.

At one moment, perched on a platform facing a packed room, Martin Launier spoke out in favor of the Marquis: "What is a republic, I ask you? The end of morality, hunting down priests, the bloody battles of 1848. Wherever there is violence and disorder, there are Républicains. I ask you, is this what we want for France? Never, never will we let them have our country!"

The applause that followed eased his worries and reassured him that they would win this election.

On February 8, he was proven right. The majority of voters agreed with the Royalists. In Poitiers, the Marquis de Chauvigny was elected, defeating Maître Lomet. The Royalists did not have an overwhelming majority, but it was enough to win.

After the election results were announced, the Launiers returned home more ecstatic than ever. They didn't even notice that Blanche and the de Marcillats had lingered behind. During the whole campaign, Blanche had not been able to kiss Gilles even one time, although she had attended several assemblies of the Républicains just to see him, without letting her parents know, of course.

While Martin Launier opened a bottle of cognac with the Marquis de Chauvigny to celebrate their victory,

Blanche took refuge in her room, secretly hoping deep down that her parents would return to Paris for good.

At the Lomet household, this win by the Royalists was not too discouraging. They had put up a good fight! And, after all, nothing was really decided yet. After Adolphe Thiers was elected Chief Executive of the new government, the National Assembly decided, in Bordeaux in March of 1871, to suspend the question of what kind of government France should embrace.

〜

The Paris Commune: March-May 1871

As the Prussian army laid siege to Paris, local markets with little to sell were unable to feed the city's inhabitants and famine began to spread. Hungry Parisians were reduced to killing cats, dogs, rats, and even the zoo animals from the Jardin des Plantes, for sustenance. Cold winter temperatures accentuated the suffering. The humiliation of surrendering Paris and fears of a reestablishment of the monarchy after the National Assembly elections led desperate Parisians to revolt.

The insurrection began on March 18, when Adolphe Thiers, then Chief Executive of France, realized that things were coming to a head and decided to take control of the cannons situated in Belleville and Montmartre.

The sight of troops marching drew a crowd, and the soldiers, who were regular Parisians, intermingled with them. Everyone agreed, Paris needed to keep its cannons in order to defend itself, not hand them over to this provisional government. The two generals charged with retrieving the cannons and bringing them to Thiers, Général Lecomte and Général Thomas, were executed by the insurgents.

Thiers, realizing what was happening, decided to move his conservative government to Versailles.

This riot led to what is called the Paris Commune, a revolutionary government that seized power in Paris for two months. A committee formed by the National Guard elected a General Council for the Commune of Paris composed of ninety members. Among them were die-hard revolutionaries, like Delescluze and Vallès, radical socialists like Ferré, Rigault, and Vaillant, workers' rights activists like Eugène Varlin, and about twenty moderates.

The Commune's first action was to adopt a red flag and to declare the absolute separation of church and state. It also announced that government employees would eventually be elected. Some of its most radical decrees included forbidding child labor for children under the age of thirteen, making overnight work illegal, and limiting the work day to ten hours. But there were weaknesses in its plan to defend the city. The Commune's generals, Rossel, Bergeret, and Cluseret, were only able to muster 30,000 men, brave men to be sure but untrained. They were no match for the

Versailles government which controlled an army of 130,000 troops led by MacMahon and stationed at the Satory camp.

MacMahon's troops entered Paris on May 21 through the Point-du-Jour gate, and the fighting was merciless on both sides. Battles broke out everywhere, though mostly in the center of Paris and on the eastern edge of the city. The last pockets of resistance were in Belleville and Père-Lachaise.

There were deaths in both camps. Any Communard bearing arms was immediately gunned down. On their side, the Communards began to execute priests, including Monsignor Darboy, the archbishop of Paris, who was trying to advocate for reconciliation. They also went after judges and other government employees who favored the old guard. When it seemed that they might be losing the fight, the Communards attacked symbolic buildings and monuments in Paris. They set fire to the Tuileries palace, the Auditor General's office, and the Hôtel de Ville, Paris' magnificent city hall.

Finally, after two months of fighting, the conservative national government defeated the Paris Commune. There were 40,000 arrests, with 270 people sentenced to death, 410 sent to work camps, 3,000 imprisoned, and 7,500 deported to the French territory of New Caledonia.

During the time that the Commune held Paris, Thiers had contacted other government leaders in Europe pleading for intervention to end the war with Prussia, and on May 10, 1871, he signed the Treaty of

Frankfurt with the Prussian kaiser. The Prussians agreed to leave France in exchange for six billion gold francs and the concession of the entire region of Alsace and a third of the Lorraine region.

So many deaths plus all of that territory in eastern France, what a price to pay!

While Paris was experiencing all of this turmoil, in the countryside, and in smaller cities like Poitiers, life carried on as usual. In the de Marcillat household, everyone was just waiting.

Ever since Martin Launier had lost his job as tutor to the Emperor's son, he had tried to regain his position as a teacher in the high school. But, people were wary about hiring someone so aligned with the empire, so vocal about his political opinions, which were Royalist or Imperialist, but never Républicain.

Everything was in a holding pattern. People in the Poitou region were aware of the confrontation between Thiers and the people of Paris.

The school was waiting to see what would happen.

The prefect was waiting to see what would happen.

The bishop was waiting to see what would happen.

Everyone plodded along, but Launier was not rehired as a teacher.

When the end of the Paris Commune was announced on May 28, 1871, Martin Launier declared that he and his wife would return to Paris the following week so that he could finish and defend his thesis at the

Sorbonne. It was decided that Honoré, who was then twenty-three years old, would stay in Poitiers to study law. Blanche could finally breathe again!

Martin Launier returned to Paris with his wife and was happy to see that Royalists were back in charge of the government. Now, he could focus on his thesis. In the political sphere, things had started to calm down, but just to be sure, Martin chose a thesis director who was generally well respected by all. Professor Pierre Duchemin had supported the Empire and was even an old friend of the former Emperor himself. Recently, he had become a Royalist and had been elected to the National Assembly. Martin was completely content with his choice and was sure there would be no problems when he defended his thesis.

Through Pierre Duchemin, Martin Launier was able to keep apprised of what was happening in the upper echelons of the government. He was still determined to become dean of the Faculté des Lettres in Poitiers one day, and to get there, he knew he would need the Royalists to retain power in the country. So, through his thesis director, he kept tabs on what was going on.

For the moment, everyone was focused on drama within the court, rather than real political issues. There were two rivals for the throne, and the Royalists were divided: some supported the grandson of Charles X, the Comte de Chambord, while others championed the grandson of Louis-Philippe, the Comte de Paris.

There were endless speeches, and both sides were hungry for power. Cartoonists lashed out with their pens, and people began to mock the rival royal counts. A decision needed to be made, and quickly. In the end, a solution was proposed. Since the Comte de Chambord had no heirs, he would be the first to reign, and the Comte de Paris would succeed him. Martin Launier was relieved. That day, he completed an entire chapter of the six chapters that would form his thesis. Everything seemed to be looking up. So, he took a first step in advancing his career by requesting a meeting with the Duc de Landry. A close friend of one of the government ministers, he was someone it would be good to know.

The Duc de Landry agreed and accepted Martin Launier's invitation for dinner. The two men found that they had a lot in common. Martin Launier had been right, the Duc de Landry was a smart connection to have. And so, the two became friends.

The political situation, however, was not completely resolved. New problems arose concerning the succession plan. The majority of Royalists were moderates and were hoping for a constitutional monarchy like the one in England. So, they needed a king who would be flexible and willing to accept a reduction in power.

Alas, the Comte de Chambord was a rather rigid man who had no interest in this type of government. He wanted a return to an absolute monarchy in France and nothing else. To make this point clear, his first act would be to reinstate the white flag of the monarchy. The Royalists were at an impasse. The National Assembly had hoped to galvanize the country around one democratic king, but it was not happening. There were more speeches and negotiations in the hope that the Comte de Chambord would come around to their thinking.

Martin Launier was sure that it would all end in some type of agreement.

During the last election cycle, Gilles Lomet had realized all that was separating him from the one he loved. Of course, he did not get involved in the struggle, but he was a Républicain and his father was fighting with all his might for the Republic. Worst of all, during the campaign, Blanche's father had become an even closer friend and confidant of the Marquis de Chauvigny, who was his own father's worst enemy. He felt like a thief, only able to steal secret moments here and there with his beloved Blanche.

Blanche never spoke of her love for Gilles to her parents when they were in Poitiers. It really was not ever the right time. The day that she showed up to meet Gilles at the courthouse, he knew right away that something good had happened. And he was right: Blanche's parents had left for Paris. For how long? A year. That would give them plenty of time to be together and to be happy again! Blanche informed him that her father planned to defend his thesis in June of 1872 and then return to be appointed Professor at the Faculté des Lettres in Poitiers.

He wondered why Blanche hadn't just come to see him at his parents' house that day? "There was too much brouhaha during the elections. My parents are so dead set against your family. It's better if we just meet in secret."

That very day, Gilles Lomet decided to leave his parents' home and rent a small house on Rue des Écossais, close to Rue de la Visitation. From then on, Blanche would go to meet him there every afternoon at five o'clock.

In the de Marcillat household, Letizia and Louis were slowly recovering from the crazy spin brought on by the extended stay of their daughter and son-in-law. For the entire election period, their home had never been empty. Now that they were gone, the two could enjoy some peace and quiet. They were not young anymore: Louis was seventy-one and Letizia sixty-six. All of the hubbub in the house was tiring. They were happy to be alone again with Blanche and with their grandson, who kept to himself and was no bother at all.

They did have one reason to worry, though. When Henriette and Martin were there, being around them, hearing them every day, they realized even more than Gilles what was separating their little Blanche from being with the man she loved. The two grandparents talked about it often, trying to figure out a way to help them.

"These things will pass," said Louis, "We don't have these kinds of elections every day."

"Yes, but our daughter and son-in-law are such fanatics."

"Martin is more Royalist than the king, for sure."

"And Henriette...they are quite a pair."

"We should talk to them about it and advocate for Gilles Lomet."

"You know quite well that Martin Launier only cares about one thing, his career."

Louis was sure that, in the long run, everything would work out. Letizia, however, was much less optimistic. More intuitive, she felt that the future for Blanche and Gilles looked bleak. She knew they were happy as long as her daughter was far away. And she let them enjoy the time they had to spend together, pretending not to notice when Blanche went out or came home late.

That winter, all of France was frozen, with cold temperatures and snowstorms the likes of which had not been seen in years. From December to February, snow blanketed the region from Poitiers to Limoges. The roads had become treacherous, carriages and stage-coaches were tipping over due to icy patches, injuring many horses that then had to be put down. They had lost track of the number of accidents.

At the highest level of government, the minister of the postal system had decided that postal carriages would deliver mail to even the most remote locations, no matter the weather and despite protests from the mail carriers who were asking for a break.

In Poitiers, not a single carriage was in the streets. Street cleaners could not keep up with the snowfall, shoveling it into carts that they would haul out of the city and dump into a field.

People trudged carefully through the snow, eyes to the ground to avoid slipping on the ice, but they still slipped on it anyway. There were innumerable falls and visits to the doctors at the Hôtel-Dieu for broken bones and sprains. The hospital beds were filling up. Some of the injured and sick were put in the old prefecture building, still empty since the opening of the new one.

When March came around, the snow melted, creating a muddy mess in the streets. Despite the mud, the city of Poitiers started to come back to life. Everyone's joy was short-lived, however, as torrential rains next battered the region. People wondered why the clouds seemed to gather so densely over the city. It rained and rained. They really thought it might never end. From the train station all the way to the Porte de Paris, the entire lower city was inundated.

Rescuers in boats helped people escape the endlessly rising waters. Some refused to leave their homes, moving up one floor and then the next, until they were living in the attic. The floods were the city's primary focus and were all anyone was talking about. Deep in the fog of young love, Blanche and Gilles Lomet barely noticed the rainstorms. They were together, no matter the weather.

It's hard to say whether there was a spring that year, but suddenly it was summer. It tiptoed in quietly, inspiring our young lovers to take long walks along the Clain River, which had finally receded. Hand in hand, in the evening, they would walk along the banks from Pont Joubert to Pont Saint-Cyprien, making plans for their future together. Their love had grown, and Gilles felt it was time:

"*Chérie*, it is time to think about getting married."

"*Grand-maman* told me that we should wait."

"But why wait?"

"She needs to be the one to tell my parents about us."

"She promised she would do so."

"My father is in the middle of his thesis. Once he's finished with it, she will talk to him."

"There's always some reason to put it off. Don't you want to marry me?"

Oh, yes! Blanche certainly did want to marry him. She hugged him tightly, and he could feel his heart begin to beat more rapidly, as it did whenever they spoke of their future together. His cheeks reddened with anger whenever she spoke of her parents. Why even ask their permission? As long as the grandparents approved...

Blanche recounted a story that her grandmother had told her about her parents. She said that they agreed to allow her mother to marry her father not just because they were in love, and not just because her father was a Royalist, but because he was a teacher at the Royal Academy.

"*Grand-maman* said that no matter what might happen, my mother's financial situation would always be stable."

"But I make a very good living, your grandparents know that. I even met your grandfather recently when my father sent me to work on an important case with him."

"He's an amazing man, isn't he?"

"Yes, and very practical."

"I just don't understand my parents. I sometimes wonder how it's possible that I am their daughter. We just have nothing in common. All they care about is politics. And I don't care one bit about it."

In fact, that very day, Martin Launier was meeting with the Duc de Landry. Not a week would go by that the two didn't share a meal together. Martin had not yet broached the topic that he really wanted to discuss. But now seemed to be the perfect time.

"After I finish my thesis, I'd like to teach at a university."

"In Paris?"

"No, in Poitiers. My goal is to become a professor in the Faculté des Lettres. The only problem is that I have no connections there."

"*Mon ami*, my dear friend, you know that you can count on me. Let me contact the dean there, Adrien. I went to university with him, and we were great friends. He would never refuse such a request from me."

And so, as soon as he had defended his thesis, Martin Launier was named professor of literature in the Faculté des Lettres in Poitiers.

∿

July 8, 1872

One sweltering summer day, Martin and Henriette Launier returned to Poitiers. In addition to all of the luggage they brought back with them were scores of items they had purchased in Paris. It was clear that they were not planning to return to the capital.

The day they arrived, Blanche went with the staff to meet them at the train station. She could think of only one thing: telling them about Gilles. She had hoped that now that the elections were long over—it had been fifteen months already—and that her father's thesis defense had gone well, they might have softened a bit.

Blanche had made the most of her time with Gilles the week before their return, as if she feared deep inside that it all might come to an end. Gilles had even taken her to the beach in La Rochelle.

Her mother and father got off the train, tired but in good spirits. They were happy to be back in Poitiers. Now that Martin was a professor at the Faculté des Lettres, everything was perfect. Blanche thought to herself that, since everything was going so well, perhaps it was indeed time for her to build a life of her own, to get married. Gilles would have to come to the house and ask for her hand in marriage.

Letizia and Louis had not gone to the train station to welcome their daughter and son-in-law. Just the thought of them being back in the house made them feel exhausted. For thirteen years, they had lived a quiet, comfortable life with Blanche, and now once again, the house would be full. The last time they stayed in Poitiers was quite stressful. Would Henriette and Martin start stirring everything up again?

At the train station, the household staff filled three carriages with all of the luggage and belongings, while the Launier family climbed into the fourth. They all returned to 21 Rue de la Visitation.

While her parents were busy unloading and unpacking, Blanche slipped away to meet Gilles at his father's law office.

"They are in such a good mood. My father has been appointed as a professor at the Faculté des Lettres. Come talk to them tomorrow!"

"I'll be there at four o'clock. Let them know that someone is coming to talk to them, but don't tell them my name. It will be a surprise."

That evening at dinner, Blanche announced to her parents, in the most neutral tone she could muster, that someone wanted to speak with them about her. Although they peppered her with questions, that's all she said.

Afterwards, her parents spent the evening listing the names of all of the young men they knew, although they realized that they didn't know very many. Someone was coming to ask for her hand in marriage, that must be it. Blanche was going to get married, and it was wonderful! And so unexpected. She was twenty-three, after all. They had forgotten. They hadn't really seen her grow up, and now they were full of ideas.

While Martin Launier listed one by one each of the important people they should invite to the wedding, Henriette began dreaming about the design of the dress she would order for Blanche. Their daughter had to make them look good. They would also have to think about a dowry. That was the least exciting part.

The next day, Henriette Launier was all dressed up. Someone was coming to ask permission to marry her daughter! She barked one order after another to the household staff, contradicting herself several times. She took out her most beautiful Parisian dress, selected a suit for her husband, demanded that her son be there even if he had to miss a class, and tried to pump her mother for information. She had no doubt that her mother knew more than she was saying.

Who would the suitor's parents be? For, surely, his parents would have to accompany him. Who would be behind that door at four o'clock? She was simply dying to know.

Hearing her parents so excited about the impending visitor, Blanche regained her confidence. As far as she could tell, her parents were as happy about this as she was. They were also thinking about her future; they also wanted her to get married. She decided to wear the dress that Gilles liked best on her.

Meanwhile, Letizia and Louis were discussing the matter in the salon.

"You are worried for no reason, my dear Letizia. Don't you see that our daughter and her husband want nothing more than a husband for Blanche?"

"The day is still young."

And the day was still young. By three o'clock, the entire family had assembled in the salon. Henriette Launier had ordered some of the delicious confections from Dufour that the whole city was raving about. On her request, the chef had prepared a charlotte, her favorite type of cake. And since she liked it, she never imagined that anyone else might not.

When they heard knocking on the door at four o'clock on the dot, they all held their breath. Valentin Durieu opened the door and ushered in a tall young man, impeccably dressed, followed by an enormous floral arrangement that the coachman set down in the entryway.

Martin Launier stood, but like his wife, was a bit disappointed. Was this all? Where were the young man's parents?

"Have your parents been delayed?"

"That's correct."

"What a pity!" cried Henriette, who gathered herself together. "Please, come in."

After kissing her hand, Gilles headed towards Letizia de Marcillat, whom he knew, and kissed her hand as well. He then shook hands with Louis. He was happy to see them there.

Once the greetings were finished, they all sat down. Henriette Launier had one question buzzing in her head: this young man looked respectable, he obviously knew her parents, but who was he? Was anyone ever going to ask for his name?

Gilles was not in a hurry to introduce himself. He had prepared a whole speech, but in the end, he just said this: "I love Blanche, and I am here to ask for her hand in marriage."

For the past day, this was all Henriette had dreamt of hearing. And hearing it, she felt as happy as the day her own husband had asked that question twenty-five years ago. What a day!

"Open the champagne!" her husband said.

As the glasses were being passed around, Henriette Launier, who was just dying to know the young man's name, dared to ask the question.

"I'm sorry, we've just returned to Poitiers after thirteen years in Paris. Your face seems familiar, but could you please remind me of your name?"

"Gilles Lomet."

"Lomet, Lomet, which Lomet family is that?"

"I am the son of Maître Jacob Lomet."

Suddenly, disaster had struck! Henriette, who really almost fainted, called for her smelling salts. Martin, whose face turned an unnatural shade of purple, seemed positively apoplectic.

"How dare you!" Martin snapped.

"In our house, our daughter Blanche!" Henriette gasped.

"Never, hear me now, never will you marry our daughter. Get out! And don't ever come back!"

Gilles left. It was as if a tornado had hit the house. Blanche's parents were beside themselves. Martin Launier was screaming that his career would be ruined if anyone important ever found out about Blanche's scandalous relationship with that man.

Henriette Launier lashed out at her daughter, calling her a slut and a hussy, and also at her mother, unable to hold back her vitriol any longer:

"You knew about it; you've known about it all along. And don't tell me that you didn't realize how bad this would be for us!"

Blanche's parents remained fully enraged for several days. To keep the peace, and so they wouldn't have to justify their behavior, Letizia and Louis didn't leave their suite, not even to come down and eat. They decided to wait it out.

Blanche was forbidden to leave the house and told to stay in her room until further notice. But when Martin Launier was at the university, she would sneak into her grandparents' quarters. Her mother noticed and tried to stop her, but this time Letizia de Marcillat took a stand and raised her voice to her daughter, something she hadn't done in a very long time.

"You will not stop me from seeing my granddaughter in my own home. Listen to me, child, you will not tell me what to do."

"If I had known that such a thing might happen one day, I would have taken Blanche to Paris with me. You let her get away with everything."

"Lower your voice, please. You are under my roof. Do I need to remind you of that? If you disagree with my decisions, you can leave. I won't stop you."

"Are you trying to say that my daughter's life is none of my business?"

"You haven't cared much about it recently. And why do you feel you are in charge of everything in my house? Blanche can come see me as often as she'd like. That's my final word, Henriette."

Letizia was relieved to have finally stood up to her daughter and wished she could do the same to her son-in-law. How could they have been so stupid as to send Maître Lomet away! It's not like suitors were banging down the door. Would poor Blanche be destined to grow old alone because of their foolishness? Henriette was a self-important idiot. It was pride that made her and her husband refuse such a good match. Plus, he was the man that Blanche loved. Letizia de Marcillat found them unbearable, but she would no longer tolerate anger and shouting in her house. In the days that followed this altercation, she felt a nagging tightness in her chest. On the fourth day, she collapsed.

As for Blanche, she had her first asthma attack the night that Gilles was sent away.

～

July 11, 1872: A letter

Gilles Lomet, Esquire
31 Rue des Écossais
Poitiers, France

July 11, 1872

Dear Madame and Monsieur Launier,

My presence in your home angered you on Sunday. I understand. You were caught by surprise, and Blanche and I should have prepared you. I alone am responsible for that decision.

It is true that our two families disagree when it comes to politics. But there is more to life than politics, and although I am a Républicain like my father, I am not a fanatic, and I can appreciate the value of those who do not share my views. Not everything should be filtered through a political lens. There is more to life, and in this life, Blanche and I are in love.

Your daughter means everything to me. I love her more than anything else in the world, and she loves me too. I want her to be my wife, and she wants me to be her husband. No one can dispute that.

I have everything she will need to be happy. I have a good job; I'm a lawyer, and I've already won some challenging cases. Monsieur de Marcillat can confirm this, as he knows me. He knows that I have a good clientele. In the future, I will be taking over my father's law firm, as I am an only child. And his firm is the best one in the city, you can ask around. I will be able to give Blanche a comfortable life and can assure you that our children and grandchildren will be well taken care of... I'm sure this is important to you.

I know that you love your daughter and that you want her to be happy; I can make her happy.

It should go without saying that I love Blanche for who she is, and I have no interest in receiving a dowry. Keep the money for her brother, who I believe will need it if he wants to establish himself as a lawyer after he finishes his studies. Further, once he passes the bar, my father and I would be happy to have him join our firm.

I'm a little older than Blanche, this is true, but I am in excellent health and engage in outdoor activities on a regular basis. I ride and hunt during hunting season, and I go swimming at the seashore when the weather permits. There are no health defects in our family. My grandparents, on both my mother's and my father's side, are all still alive. My maternal grandmother is seventy-eight years old and her husband is eighty, and my paternal grandfather is eighty-six and his wife is seventy. All four are quite healthy. The same goes for my parents. May God allow them long lives as well!

It is true that we are Protestant and you are Catholic. But the religious wars are far in the past, let's not revive them. As far as the education of our future children is concerned, Blanche will not be required to raise them as Protestants. We will do whatever she chooses. You see that I am no extremist when it comes to religion either. As for the wedding, I'd agree to have it in a Catholic church even though I am devoutly Protestant. Do you think I would agree to all of these things if I didn't truly love Blanche? I hope that you now see that you can trust me, and you will give me permission to marry her.

There is no reason to oppose this marriage. Let your daughter live her life, respect her feelings, give me her hand in marriage, I beg of you. I will be the son-in-law that you want me to be.

Sincerely yours,
Gilles Lomet

Martin Launier responded quickly. Short, but clear, his message extinguished all hope for the young lovers. Gilles Lomet read it in silence; deep inside, he could not believe what he was reading.

July 29, 1872

Monsieur,
Please stop bothering us and stay away from our daughter.
My answer is no and will always be no.
Respectfully,
Martin Launier

IV

1872

Letizia de Marcillat was hospitalized at the Hôtel-Dieu until August. Her daughter and granddaughter would come visit her every day. Her son-in-law came once a week, on Sundays. Louis de Marcillat had requested a bed be set up for him right next to her. He never left her side. The nurses insisted that their patient needed rest, so the visits were always very short. She was slowly improving, they would say, from an intense emotional episode.

When they were with her, Blanche and Henriette acted as if they had reconciled. In reality, they hadn't. They pretended to be getting along for the benefit of Letizia de Marcillat and the hospital staff. Henriette Launier insisted that the family appear to be unified to outsiders. Of course, she did not feel any responsibility for her mother's illness. So, when the doctor in the cardiology unit pulled her aside to ask what had happened to send her mother into such a state, she hesitated a moment and said: "Her only granddaughter upset her quite terribly. The girl stated her desire to marry someone that her grandmother does not approve of. It was simply too much for her."

Obviously, when she told the doctor this, Blanche was not with her. The doctor asked to speak with Blanche and gave her the following advice: "The most important thing is to not disagree with your grandmother right now. Until she is fully recovered, just agree with whatever she says."

Blanche promised to do so.

Henriette Launier knew that no one would discover her lie. Her mother was not the type of person to discuss private matters in public. So, for the moment, she could sleep peacefully and continue to put pressure on her daughter. From that time on, Blanche was no longer allowed to go out unaccompanied. She had to be with her mother or her father. In the beginning, she made an attempt to go out with one or the other, hoping to at least catch a glimpse of Gilles, but reality soon hit home. Her mother rarely went out, apart from visits to the Hôtel-Dieu hospital, and her father never went out except to go to work.

While Letizia de Marcillat was in the hospital, there were few visitors to 21 Rue de la Visitation. The director of the medical school, Pierre Bauché, and the old dean of the Faculté des Lettres, Adrien de Fresnay, would come for dinner once a week, but that was it. The lively gatherings her grandparents used to organize were no more. The house had become a dreary place.

Blanche wanted to play piano in the mornings, as she used to, but her mother opposed: "You want to play music while your grandmother is so sick? And you say you love her. You clearly have no feeling in your heart."

Shortly thereafter, Mademoiselle Ursule Manin, Blanche's music instructor, was told her services were no longer required. Blanche had to give up singing and playing piano. With nothing to do, she would just wander from one room to another in the expansive mansion, perhaps stopping to chat with Céline Thébaud, the cook who had known her since she was little.

She could still tend to her turtledoves in the garden, but that didn't take up too much time. She could also work on her embroidery, though she hated it; or she could read, but she never felt like it. She used to go read in her grandparents' library, while her grandmother painted watercolors and her grandfather developed his photographs. She missed them terribly. Life with her parents, who didn't understand her at all, was stifling. She would often just hole up in her room, a place her mother never set foot. There, she would write letters to Gilles. Every day, she would pass a letter to Émilie Frasié, her grandparents' housekeeper. Émilie knew about her love for Gilles and would discreetly deliver the letters to him.

Preoccupied by her mother's illness, Henriette Launier had no idea this was happening.

Blanche and Gilles promised each other that they would love each other forever, but their lives seemed to have come to a halt. She couldn't wait for her grandparents to come back home. In order to avoid suspicion, Blanche would come down to eat with her parents at mealtimes, forcing herself to behave. She said yes to everything and patiently awaited her grandmother's recovery.

When Letizia de Marcillat started to feel a little better, she returned home. The ride home was a bit tiring, for it was a hot and humid day. Louis was coming home with her after five weeks in the hospital. It had also been exactly five weeks since Blanche and her grandmother had been able to talk privately. When she saw her grandmother in the doorway, Blanche felt a wave of happiness come over her; finally, things would go back to how they were, before her parents had returned to Poitiers. Her father wanted to become a dean. Who knows, maybe he would be appointed to a university in another city?

Although he did dream of becoming a dean, Martin Launier wanted, in particular, to become a dean in Poitiers; that was what he had requested of the Duc de Landry. It was no coincidence that the current elderly dean, Adrien de Fresnay, was regularly invited to dinner. And Martin's plan was working, for Adrien de Fresnay held him in his highest regard. Someone who had been the private tutor to the Emperor's son would be an ideal successor, and he had made his opinion quite clear.

Being away for a time, Letizia de Marcillat had been able to forget all of the things that had been troubling her: Blanche's future, her feelings rejected, and the damage that her daughter and son-in-law had done by refusing the marriage proposal. Now that she was back home, she realized that the problem had not resolved itself. Henriette and Martin would not let it go. And in case she had any hopes to the contrary, her daughter was there to bring her back to reality. Henriette curtly summarized the reply that her husband had written to Gilles Lomet's letter and declared the matter closed. She said that Blanche was taking it very well and that Letizia should not continue to fill the girl's head with nonsense.

But as soon as Blanche was alone with her *grand-maman*, she told her about her secret correspondence with Gilles. Letizia realized how blind her daughter was, but she felt tired and old. With this illness, it seemed that death had put her on notice. She decided to make good use of the time she had left. So, without a second thought, she resolved to assist Blanche. She would need to be careful and cunning. "Let me take care of it," she said to her granddaughter, "now let's go out for a walk."

From then on, the two would spend every afternoon strolling through Blossac Park, rain or shine. Knowing how her daughter thought, the first few days, they went by way of Boulevard de la Gare. She was smart to do this, as Henriette had made Marie Pinaud follow them to find out where they were going and to make sure they weren't going to Gilles Lomet's house. After a few weeks, feeling confident that nothing was going on, she told the maid to stop her surveillance of the pair and stay at home.

That's when the old woman changed their route and started to take Rue des Écossais to get to the park. There, Blanche would meet up with Gilles. Once a week, taking the precaution of changing days now and then, she would leave them alone for several hours. She would wait on a nearby bench until Blanche would come join her, and then side by side, they would return to Rue de la Visitation.

Blanche's brother Honoré was in the process of completing his thesis to obtain a doctorate in law. He had chosen as his topic the idea of "complicity."

He loved his sister, although they had been separated for thirteen years while he was in Paris with his parents. From time to time, he would go visit her in her room. During those talks, she would explain all of her woes. They were just one year apart in age, and they looked so similar, one might think they were twins. But they were of two different minds. Honoré thought solely of his career, while Blanche thought solely of her feelings. He was completing graduate school, while she had attended the local parochial school run by Ursuline nuns, and she had stopped going there at age fifteen. Blanche had been taught how to behave well in society, while Honoré had learned how to influence society. There was a deep divide between them. One trusted sound reasoning and nothing else, while the other trusted only her heart. They did not see eye to eye.

Honoré did not have a girlfriend, and in fact, he never even thought about relationships. All he wanted was to obtain a good position in the government, everything else would come later. His dream was to become an important government official, a prefect! While he hadn't yet completed his thesis, his father had already planted the seed in his longstanding correspondence with the Duc de Landry. Although they no longer lived near each other, they remained close friends. As long as the Royalists continued to control the country, a position for Honoré was pretty much guaranteed. They just needed the Républicains to stay quiet. Like his parents, Honoré considered the Lomet family as enemies who had to be prevented from doing harm to the nation.

He advised his sister to forget about Gilles, to focus her time on painting, embroidery, anything other than love. He was also one of those people who worried about what people might think, and he was heavily influenced by his mother. The Launiers had invested all of their hopes and dreams in him. At least he would be able to give them some satisfaction. At the university, he only ever associated himself with other Royalists. He was a good son.

Blanche spoke with him about how much she was suffering, but knowing how close her brother was to their mother, she made sure not to mention that she was still in contact with Gilles, that she was more in love than ever, and that he felt the same. Honoré found his sister to be quite fanciful, like a heroine from a novel, except he wasn't a big reader and had no idea how to cheer her up. Whenever he went to visit her, it was usually so that he could talk about himself. It was a topic he found particularly interesting. Their conversations never lasted very long, and Blanche knew that their mother would try to get information out of him afterwards, so she never told him too much. She even sometimes suspected that he had been sent there by her mother to find out what she was thinking, so she often played the role of a happy young woman just to keep the peace.

Henriette Launier never did actually send Honoré to Blanche's room; he went on his own accord. But he was so much like his parents that he couldn't comprehend her passion for Gilles, or any passion for that matter. Henriette, having complete faith in her son, agreed to allow him to take Blanche to Blossac Park for walks. Blanche went with him a few times, but these walks didn't help at all. She even felt like more of a prisoner out with him than at home alone in her room.

Obviously, Blanche was no longer allowed to go to the Palais de Justice. It was her brother who asked the question, though her mother had often wondered herself: "How exactly did you meet Gilles Lomet?" She explained: "At the first trial I attended, when I was fifteen. After that, *grand-maman* and I would go to the courthouse almost every day." Her explanation was later repeated to her mother who was convinced more than ever of the deleterious role the grandmother had played in this unseemly relationship. From then on, no more trials for Blanche!

When she wasn't in her room, she could usually be found in her grandparents' suite. They occupied the right wing of the mansion, and she still confided in *grand-maman*. She would ask all sorts of questions, getting her to talk, searching her past for clues to what the future might hold. In particular, she never tired of hearing Letizia tell the story of how she met Louis.

"Your grandfather was just an unknown stockbroker, but the day he set foot in our house, I knew right away that he was the only one for me."

"Were your parents really opposed to your marriage?"

"Yes, your *grand-papa* had no money, no family fortune. All he had was his family name: de Marcillat. My parents wanted me to marry a wealthy man."

"Tell me again how it happened!"

"I had packed up all of my things. I told the coachman that father was sending me to Louis' house and asked him to fetch a carriage. Once I arrived at your grandfather's place, I refused to leave and stayed the whole night. My parents were so worried about a scandal that they finally gave in. The next day, they gave him permission to marry me."

"But, *grand-maman*, Gilles is a lawyer. He wouldn't want a marriage built on a scandal."

"My dear, wait until you are twenty-five, after that no one can stop you from marrying him. You just have to send your parents a legal notice. Since there seems to be no other way, that's what you must do."

Full of hope that they would be reunited when Blanche turned twenty-five—in just one year—the two lovers decided to wait it out.

Émilie Frasié had resumed working for the de Marcillats. While Letizia was in the hospital, she had taken orders from Henriette Launier, but she disliked Henriette, whom she found to be quite pretentious. She was completely devoted to the de Marcillats, however, having served them since she was thirteen years old.

When Letizia de Marcillat was too tired to go out with her granddaughter, it was Émilie who played postman and delivered Blanche's letters to Gilles Lomet. So, Blanche had three accomplices in the house: her two grandparents, especially her *grand-maman*, and Émilie Frasié.

One beautiful day in June, Honoré defended his thesis. As expected, he passed "with distinction." But he had little time to rest on his laurels because the post his father had requested for him was soon announced. As a starting position, while he waited to be appointed prefect, he was named as legal advisor for the prefecture of Mont-de-Marsan. Like all good government workers, he had to start somewhere and then work his way up.

Blanche felt rather indifferent about her brother's defense of his doctoral thesis in law. She was neither happy nor sad, and seemed unaffected by his impending departure for the South of France. On the day he left, he said a tender goodbye to his sister, promising that she could come visit him as soon as he was settled and hinting that she might soon have a wedding to attend, for he had decided to start looking for a wife.

Honoré had indeed begun to think seriously about marriage. Just as he had planned out his studies, he started to plan out his married life. Without a wife, it would surely be more difficult to obtain promotions. A beautiful wife to entertain guests and to draw attention to him, that's what was needed. He arrived in the South of France determined to find his perfect match. Mediterranean women were just his type, so he was sure he'd find the right match in the South of France.

Louis and Letizia de Marcillat were very happy for Honoré the day he defended his thesis. His future prospects were bright and success nearly guaranteed. That said, they were not really sad to see him leave. They had never been very close with their grandson. They were happy for his success and his new career, but that was about it.

As Letizia kissed him goodbye, she felt a little tug in her heart that told her she might not live long enough to see him again. Honoré loved his grandmother, whom he found to be quite beautiful. The thought that he might not see her again had never crossed his mind. After she returned from bidding him farewell at the train station, she hugged her husband Louis as tightly as she could. She loved him more than anything in the world. For the first time, she wondered what might become of him if she died.

That afternoon, she confided in Blanche:

"You know that I could die."

"No, you are far too young for that, *grand-maman*!"

"I will die one day, and it might be soon."

"If you die, what will become of us, of *grand-papa* and me? Have you thought about that?"

"Indeed, if anything were to happen, you must promise me one thing."

"What's that?"

"Promise me that you will take care of your grandfather."

Blanche promised to fulfill her grandmother's wishes, though she could not imagine her world without her. She was such a big part of her life; she had always been there for her. That night, she was filled with anxiety and had a terrible asthma attack.

∽

August 1873

One evening, Letizia de Marcillat was feeling more tired than usual. Typically, after having supper in the dining room, she and her husband would retire to their suite. But, that night, she took Blanche's arm and led her out into the garden.

The two of them, seated on a swing, breathed in the strong scent of summer flowers in bloom.

"Do you still love Gilles?"

"Only seven more months, *grand-maman*, and we can be married. I've been waiting a long time, and the longer I wait, the further away it seems."

"Your heart has been constant. Never give up on him, no matter what happens."

"No, I would never! We love each other. Soon, you will come to our wedding. You will come, won't you?"

"Who knows? I would like to, but I'm an old woman, and I'm tired."

"You're tired because it's so hot out; the heat makes me feel fatigued as well. I'll be married in April, so it won't be as hot."

"Do you remember the promise you made me? If I die, you are to take care of your grandfather, *oui*?"

"Oh, *grand-maman*, you must keep living, for him and for me. What will become of us if you are no longer here?"

"Only God can make those decisions, my dear Blanche... I've made my will and left my fortune to you. Your grandfather will have survivor's rights, but eventually my estate will be yours. I'm also leaving you all of my jewelry. I wanted to be sure that you would have everything you need."

"I don't care about money. I need you and *grandpapa*, that's all. What will happen to me without you here?"

Gently, Letizia de Marcillat leaned on Blanche's shoulder and stood up. They went back inside, and

Blanche accompanied her grandmother up to her suite. When she got back to her room, she had a bad feeling.

The next day, Letizia de Marcillat née Békler did not wake up. Louis' desperate cries woke up the whole household. Blanche could not believe it. It wasn't possible. Everything was fine last night when they were chatting in the garden. They had even gone for a walk yesterday afternoon in Blossac Park. As usual, *grand-maman* had waited on a bench in front of the prefecture while she went to see Gilles. *Mon Dieu! Quelle horreur!* Her world was crumbling.

Émilie Frasié was put in charge of preparing the body for viewing, dressing Letizia in one of her finest gowns. The maid wept the entire time. She had a hard time separating Louis from his wife because he was still clinging to her as if she were still alive. A darkness descended on the entire household. Letizia had arrived there at the age of sixteen, a young bride, and departed at the age of sixty-eight. This passionate woman's presence, and her ability to fight for what she believed in, permeated every part of the house, including the walls, the furniture, even the stairways. Now she was gone, and the entire household mourned her loss.

Taking advantage of one brief moment when her father was at the university teaching a class and her mother was mourning at Letizia's bedside, Blanche snuck out to visit Gilles and tell him the horrible news. It was a shock for him as well. He had loved her for being their faithful ally, for caring for Blanche, for standing up to the Launiers despite her age. Because of Blanche's parents, Gilles did not go to pay his respects to Letizia on her deathbed, which was difficult for him. But he did attend the burial; no one could stop him from being there.

∿

August 31, 1873

The day they buried Letizia de Marcillat, it was stiflingly hot. At the cemetery, a silent crowd dressed in black listened to the new bishop, Paul Duillaume. He had replaced Aimé Dulaire, who had also recently passed away.

"Jesus spoke to Lazarus, Lazarus his friend, a friend who was lifeless, who everyone thought was dead, who was being mourned as we mourn Letizia today. Jesus said to Lazarus: 'Come forth!' and Lazarus stood before them, welcomed by boisterous applause and exclamations of joy. We will also hear these exclamations of joy on the day of the resurrection. For we know today that our death, the death that makes us suffer in this moment, is just a test.

"Letizia, whom we loved so dearly, you too will be resurrected! I promise you this, my brothers, just as Jesus promised us all.

"Letizia, you will be restored to your body, you will shine with the light of Christ, on the day he chooses. You were baptized in Christ and chosen to represent him on earth. You were a faithful servant, and so I say to you, Letizia, you will be seated at his right hand one day."

Blanche sobbed. She was as pale as a ghost and hadn't eaten for three days. Her mother was also crying. Although they disagreed on many things, Henriette Launier loved her mother and would have liked to have kept her with them a little longer. Blanche clung to her grandfather, who also could not stop crying.

As they lowered the casket into the ground, Louis fell on his knees. His despair was palpable. It almost seemed he was losing his mind. He banged his head on the ground. His daughter tried to get him to stand up, but he pushed her aside.

Many people had come to the burial. Everyone knew her. A lot of them had spent evenings at her house, back when she used to invite people over, back when she was younger and her daughter and son-in-law were living in Paris. Others knew her from Blossac Park.

No one noticed, but Gilles Lomet was there too. He stayed towards the back and watched Blanche from a distance. How he wished he could hold her in his arms! That's where he should be. And he remembered Letizia's advice: "Just be patient!" The time wasn't right. On that day, Blanche bore a striking resemblance to her grandmother. Seeing how broken Louis de Marcillat was, Gilles realized that things were about to change. From then on, nothing would be easy for Blanche.

People started to approach the family to pay their respects. One by one, they tried to offer small words of comfort. Several of them embraced Louis de Marcillat, who stood there motionless like a zombie. The condolences went on and on. Martin Launier and his wife struggled to hold Louis upright, for it seemed he might collapse at any moment.

Blanche had searched the crowd looking for Gilles Lomet and finally slipped off to be with him. Without a word, she threw herself into his arms. Not a soul noticed.

The household staff hurried home after the burial to set the table. The butler hung a black cloth under the portico at the main entrance to the de Marcillat mansion and draped it around the door. The family was in mourning. These cloths would remain in place for a month.

Gilles Lomet had brought Blanche home with him in his coach. He kept her with him all afternoon. No one was paying attention to her whereabouts. Her parents never even wondered where she was since they were sure that her affair with Maître Lomet was ancient history.

Very few members of the Békler family were there. The only one, really, was Letizia's brother Napoléon. He had traveled from Colmar and was a wreck when he arrived. Their parents, along with their other brothers and sisters, were all deceased. The next day, he left early to head back to eastern France.

At noon on the burial day, a meal was served for all the friends and relatives of the Launier and de Marcillat families. The food had been prepared the day before by Céline Thébaud. There were ninety place settings. They had brought the dining room table out to the garden and extended it with outdoor dining tables. They also brought out the long table from the library. Crisp, white tablecloths were draped over the tables, which were aptly decorated with small bouquets of forget-me-nots.

Although Martin Launier had loved his mother-in-law, that day, he was actually quite happy. He was in his element and loved these types of ceremonial events that reminded him of Paris and of the Empire. And his wife was just perfect: in a black crêpe dress that covered her neck, she stood as tall and straight as ever. Her hair was twisted into a neat bun, tied with a ribbon at the back. Martin and Henriette Launier drifted from one guest to the next, while everyone drank cognac and talked about all of Letizia's best qualities.

At one point, Henriette thought to go look for her daughter, but she quickly got distracted, having so many other things to do. Blanche must be somewhere in the house, wallowing in her grief, she thought to herself.

It was a lavish funeral, and the guests did not just have lunch at the mansion, they stayed for dinner. They spent the entire day in the garden. The sun was shining, and the flow of alcohol loosened people up and led to moments of laughter; if not for the dark clothing, one might have thought this a wedding celebration. Ever since the onset of her mother's illness, Henriette had been dreaming of a grand funeral celebration; one of those interments you just can't forget. She had to provide proof of her love for her mother, irrefutable and visible proof. She wanted all of Poitiers to say: "That

Henriette Launier, she really loved her mother!" And so, that's what happened.

The noon meal was fit for a king: potage Saint-Germain with fresh peas, escalope of lobster à la Parisienne, timbale of macaroni, marinated venison, assorted beans in a butter sauce, rice pudding with currants, and a decadent bombe glacée. They washed it all down with fine Algerian wine from the Domaine de Maraval. The evening meal was equally sumptuous.

Yes, it was a memorable day. Martin Launier was even able to make some new acquaintances that might be useful in his quest to become dean of the Faculté des Lettres. As for Henriette Launier, her sorrow lifted. She felt good about this very full day for which she had spared no expense.

Around five o'clock, Blanche returned home. She did not go out into the garden to speak with anyone and had no trouble making it upstairs without being noticed. She did not go to her room, however, but to her grandmother's chamber, which still smelled of incense, even though the windows had been left wide open. Her immediate thought was that her mother wanted to rid the house of her grandmother's scent. She opened Letizia's armoire and took out several dresses. Tears rolled down her cheeks as she buried her face in the fabric, hoping to smell her grandmother's perfume. She disliked hearing all of the voices and the laughter floating up from the garden. She sat down in her grandmother's favorite armchair and opened the book left there to the page she had marked. It was a collection of poems by Victor Hugo entitled *La Légende des Siècles*, and she began to read aloud as *grand-maman* used to love to do. As she spoke, she heard her grandmother's voice.

Next, she made her way over to the library. Letizia de Marcillat used to go there to read or to paint watercolors. Blanche picked up one painting after another. Some of them were portraits of her, others were paintings of animals, mostly deer, or the sea, and lots of flowers. She remembered how much her grandmother loved flowers and promised herself to put fresh flowers on her grandmother's grave every day.

She sat down in the rocking chair to think. Her grandmother had asked her to care for her grandfather, and that's what she was going to do. Earlier, in the cemetery, he could barely stand. She went to his room to make sure he had come up and gone to bed. He was there, listless, a bottle of alcohol lying next to him. He was crying. She went over to him and placed her hand on his shoulder. He brushed it aside. Blanche stepped back, for she understood; she too needed time alone to think about her. So, she went back to her own room next door.

Down in the courtyard, the party was still going on. The noisy guests were even louder now. Her room opened onto the garden, and the festivities seemed to go on and on. Several times, she thought about yelling from the window to tell them to be quiet, that *grand-maman* was dead, and that this was not a wedding reception. But she stopped herself. She felt a huge weight crushing her lungs. She was sweating and her hands were trembling. She started to cough and felt like something was caught in her throat and blocking her airway. She began wheezing... She felt like she was suffocating... All of a sudden, the room felt like it was closing in on her. She couldn't breathe. She needed air. She wanted to shout "Help! Help me!" but nothing came out. She envisioned her grandmother on her deathbed in her garnet-colored velvet dress, her long braided hair, and her hands joined together holding a string of rosary beads... And those horrible scenes of placing her in the coffin and lowering it into the ground. She was gasping for air and was afraid she might die.

That very night, provoked by these spasmodic attacks, with tears in her eyes, Blanche moved into a different room, a larger one that looked out onto the street.

During the month after Letizia's death, Blanche spent most of her time with her grandfather, who never stopped thinking about his wife.

Louis de Marcillat loved photography. As soon as the photograph was invented, he began to feed his passion for this new form of art. He had installed a darkroom near his library, and there he developed the negatives. He took photographs of everything, but Letizia was his favorite subject. Her death had been a surprise to him, as it had been to many others. So, he spent hours leafing through his photo albums; photos of her adorned nearly every page.

His grief never lessened. He rarely went out, except to visit his wife's grave with Blanche. When they arrived, Blanche would say a short prayer and lay a fresh bouquet of flowers on the ground. Then she would leave her grandfather alone. He would sit on the gravestone for some time, in silence, just thinking... During those moments, Blanche would meet up with Gilles Lomet, who would be waiting for her behind the large cypress trees. In spite of everything, they were still in love and holding out hope for better days.

When Louis de Marcillat was not at the cemetery with his granddaughter, he was in his room looking at photographs, with a bottle of alcohol by his side. There were hundreds of photos of Letizia. No matter the setting or the subject of the photograph, she was there: in the foreground, in the background, on the side, in the room, next to the Clain River, in a boat, on a horse, at the seashore...she was always there.

When Blanche was with him, he would explain why he had decided to take this photo or that. When she wasn't, particularly in the evenings, his eyes would well up and the tears would start to flow. It became common to see him with a drink in hand. Wine made him sad. And often they would find him with his head in his hands, sobbing in despair about the loss of his dear Letizia.

When Émilie Frasié would find him crying, she would try to cheer him up, but was never successful. He missed Letizia, and photographs were not enough. He just wanted her back, and no one could make that happen. Since he was older than her, he had always thought that he would die first. It never crossed his mind that it might be the other way around. He was angry at

God for separating them, for taking her away from him. When his wife was alive, he used to go to mass at the cathedral every Sunday; after her death, he stopped attending and even Blanche couldn't convince him to go.

Blanche would go to mass with her parents. She knew that Gilles would be taking his parents to their church at the same time. Thinking of the two of them, each in their own churches praying at the same time, made her feel closer to him.

Blanche always remembered to pray for her *grand-maman*.

Little by little, she started to get back to eating normally. She remained quite thin and frail, but it helped that Émilie Frasié was still there to share memories and talk about the past.

Shortly before her death, feeling that the end was near, Letizia de Marcillat had written up a new will that she had filed with Maître Billedoux, a notary and old friend of the family. He had often been a guest in their home and was among those who attended the funeral. A month after her death, the will had still not been read. Henriette Launier figured that her father was too overwrought to handle such a task that would inevitably make him more upset. Chrétien Billedoux agreed with her; they should wait until he was up to it.

The day that Louis de Marcillat ate a full meal at noon instead of just a biscuit, Henriette Launier sent Marie Pinaud to notify the notary that a meeting should be arranged as soon as possible. Henriette and Martin couldn't wait to hear what was in the will. When she was alive, they often had disagreements with her, especially towards the end when they weren't getting along at all because Letizia was so dead set on having Blanche marry that Lomet fellow. So, they worried that the will might contain some surprises. In fact, that was the case.

Maître Billedoux consented to Henriette's request and set the meeting time for the next day. Louis de Marcillat begrudgingly got dressed for the appointment. He was annoyed about having to go to the notary's office. He had asked his daughter several times whether he couldn't just stay home, but Henriette Launier was intractable. He had to go. Maître Billedoux followed the letter of the law. They all needed to be there.

The coachman prepared the carriage to take them to the notary's office. Blanche was curious to know what was in the will. Did her grandmother have a strongbox full of family secrets that might be left to her? Love letters, perhaps?

The notary began to read the will, and as Louis de Marcillat heard his wife's words, he sobbed unremittingly. His daughter looked at him with contempt. He had become a total wreck and could no longer control himself.

"I, the undersigned Letizia de Marcillat née Békler, born on August 1, 1805 in Colmar, wife of Louis de Marcillat, of sound mind and body, bequeath my entire fortune to my granddaughter Blanche..."

Henriette Launier nearly jumped out of her skin. The entire fortune to Blanche? But what about them, what about her, what would happen to them? According to the will, Louis would retain full use of the estate while he was alive. That was all well and good, but he would not live forever. He was nearing the end of his rope, that was clear. And when he died, then what would happen? Blanche could send them away. She could sell the property. It wasn't right. Her mother must have been out of her mind!

As soon as the reading of the will was over, Henriette Launier could not help but pull the notary aside to ask him what they needed to do to render this unfair document null and void. But alas, Maître Chrétien Billedoux explained to her that the will was valid and, furthermore, that there was no way around it. Furious, the Launiers returned home.

Once they were in their private suite, the rage that Henriette and Martin had been holding in began to spill out.

"My mother was a crazy old hag, and my father is losing it. What can be done?"

"Make him sign a document today giving you power of attorney."

"Yes, you're right. I should do that right away. But when he dies, what will happen to us?"

"We need to figure that out."

"Never in my lifetime will I allow this house to be sold. Blanche is just as incapable of handling her affairs as my father is. She will live here, and I will continue to be in charge."

Louis de Marcillat had been overwhelmed by the reading of his wife's will. It was not because of the contents, for he understood quite well why his wife had left everything to Blanche, it was because of hearing the words his wife had written. Those ten minutes of listening to her words being read aloud made him feel for a moment that she had been brought back to life. Afterwards, he was not the same. It was as if he was confronted with her death a second time. He refused to leave his armchair. Blanche couldn't even convince him to go to the cemetery with her. He spent hours in the library, without moving, smoking a pipe with a glass of cognac in his hand.

He no longer went downstairs at mealtime. In his room, he barely ate anything and wouldn't speak at all. Neither Blanche nor Émilie Frasié were able to get two words out of him. He closed himself off in a profound silence and sunk into the bottle. Henriette Launier couldn't take it anymore and refused to go upstairs to see him. She had her power of attorney, and that was enough. She went through all of her parents' affairs. She combed through every bit of paperwork, investments, assets, accounts, expenses incurred by their various properties. She took all of the files to her suite.

Henriette had begun to alienate the household help. She had given up on questioning her father about past expenses, and had turned on the staff, in particular on

Émilie Frasié, whom she riddled with questions that more or less conveyed her suspicions. Émilie had an unpleasant realization that she might be accused of dishonesty.

Everyone had been given notice: Henriette was now in charge. She would set the wages, and the staff would have to speak to her about any purchases. Her father was no longer capable of making such decisions. Assembled in the salon, the staff listened to her without any visible reaction. From then on, Émilie Frasié would still be assigned to Louis de Marcillat, but she would answer to Henriette Launier. Henriette reveled in her newfound authority. It had taken her a while to recover from the blow her mother had dealt her: giving everything to Blanche. You see, her mother had already been wealthy before she married Louis. The mansion they were all living in belonged to her. When they married, her father was penniless. All of the inheritances they received, which increased their fortune, came from Letizia's side of the family.

Since Blanche's grandfather no longer wanted to go to the cemetery, Blanche did not go out much either. Her parents insisted that she have a chaperone whenever she left the house, so she could no longer see Gilles Lomet. She kept writing to him every day, though, and Émilie Frasié kept delivering the letters. Their love had never been stronger. Blanche was counting the days until she was old enough to marry him. Five more months... While waiting, she passed the time with her grandfather, reading to him aloud. She also took care of her turtledoves, feeding them twice a day, and she organized photographs or spent hours trying on different dresses. She had taken possession of all of her grandmother's gowns, and some were quite beautiful. She dreamt of the day she would be able to wear them for Gilles, to make him happy. She also often tried on the jewelry that her grandmother had left her.

Her appetite had come back, and sitting in the garden in the evenings, she watched as the leaves started to turn and autumn arrived. It seemed like it would be a stormy fall, but the weather didn't bother her at all, for it was the last fall that she would spend without Gilles. Next year, she would be Madame Lomet, in God's eyes and in everyone's eyes.

She enjoyed spending time with her grandfather. Occasionally, he would break his silence. He would talk about happy times in the past. He would ask his granddaughter questions to get her to talk about their fondest memories.

"Do you remember when we saw the solar eclipse in 1860?"

"Of course, *grand-papa*! I was eleven, I remember it well. It was during the summer."

"It was in July. July 18, 1860."

"You have such a great memory, *grand-papa*!"

"Your parents were at the court of Napoléon III at that time."

"It was an incredible day. All of Poitiers was in Place d'Armes."

"All of France was watching the eclipse. You could also see it from America, from the Sahara Desert, from everywhere."

"We all waited for the sun to disappear."

"I purchased this telescope just for that day. It was my first one, the one on the table there. Tell me again what you remember."

"All of a sudden, it got dark out. You couldn't see anything at all. Everyone was exclaiming 'Oh! Ah!' like they were watching fireworks. Then everyone started clapping, and I clapped too. It was amazing."

"Yes, but what was it like? Come on, tell me!"

"It was a long time ago, *grand-papa*."

"The moon darkened, and around it was a kind of greenish glow that gave off a very soft light. You'd forgotten, eh?"

"Well, I remember that it was dark for a long time."

"No, Blanche, not for a long time. It was only ten minutes."

"I think it was longer."

"Look in the drawer there and take out my newspaper clippings from that time. You'll see that I'm right."

As evening fell, Blanche took out the old newspaper articles and read them by candlelight to please her grandfather. The old man never went out anymore, but was able to find some small happiness in spending time with his granddaughter and getting to know her better. When Letizia was alive, she was the one who usually spent time with Blanche. To entertain her *grand-papa*,

Blanche decided that the next day, or maybe the day after that, she would get dressed up in one of her grandmother's prettiest gowns and put on the jewelry she always wore. Her grandfather, hazy after several glasses of cognac, looked at her as if she were his Letizia and talked about taking her photograph.

V

Letizia de Marcillat had been gone for several months, and Blanche was getting closer to turning twenty-five. Letters were still being exchanged, thanks to Émilie Frasié. Everything was going so well, in fact, that Blanche had abandoned many of the precautions she used to take and had started reading her letters in plain sight in the garden. One day, her mother took notice. Since she was first to receive any incoming mail, she knew full well that that no letters had arrived from her son that day, and he was the only one who typically wrote to Blanche. Henriette Launier began to wonder who might be corresponding with her daughter.

Henriette quickly approached her daughter and snatched the letter out of her hands. When she realized what the letter was, she was as dumbfounded as she was furious. Her daughter was still in love with that horrible lawyer. And not only did she still love him, he returned her love, and they had been writing to each other behind her back all this time. Suddenly, she realized the full impact that this relationship might have, now that her daughter had inherited Letizia's fortune. Needing time to plot her next move, she hid her anger from her daughter and returned to the salon as if nothing had happened, to Blanche's great surprise.

As usual, Henriette Launier called for Marie Pinaud to assist her in running errands. They left the house with baskets in hand.

At lunchtime, all seemed normal, and perhaps as if Henriette had forgotten the incident. She obviously hadn't mentioned it to her husband Martin, as the conversation that day focused solely on his work at the university. After the meal was over, while the maids were clearing off the table, Blanche went to sit with her grand-father to read to him for a little while, as she often did. Next, while he was napping, she went to his library to dive into a novel herself.

That was when Henriette Launier decided to go rummage through Blanche's room. There, tied up in ribbons and interspersed with dried flower petals, she found more than two hundred love letters from Gilles Lomet! Beside herself, she took them to her own room and began to read through them voraciously. She was absolutely floored by what she learned: when her daughter turned twenty-five, she planned to run off to be with her lover, forcing them to agree to the marriage! For Henriette Launier, that meant one thing, that the mansion would soon be sold. Her father was seventy-three years old and was not well. He would soon be gone. If her daughter married, the fortune would soon be gone as well. Henriette felt that she had to take action.

First, she needed to know how the two lovebirds were able to exchange letters. Someone in the household had to be helping them. Her daughter never went out unless accompanied by herself or her husband, so she must have an accomplice. After considering every member of the staff, she concluded that it must be Émilie Frasié. She had never trusted that woman, who was always completely devoted to her mother Letizia and must have agreed with her concerning Blanche's future. Further, that woman was the one who spent the most time with Blanche, since she was assigned to tend to Louis de Marcillat.

Henriette Launier placed the letters back where she found them and, with some trepidation, closed the door to Blanche's room. She needed to know more, to be patient, so as to fully destroy her daughter's plans. For several days, she watched the maids, the gardener, the butler, the coachman. In the mornings, Émilie Frasié would go out to visit her grandson at his nanny's home, and when she returned, she'd go straight to Blanche's room. Henriette, peering through a crack in the door, witnessed her passing a letter to Blanche. Again, she didn't let on. She simply called Émilie Frasié into her office. There, Henriette unleashed her fury:

"You are acting as the go-between for my daughter and that lawyer!"

"Your mother asked me to do it."

"Don't you dare use my mother to justify your misdeeds!"

"But really, I assure you..."

"Let me be brief: you will immediately stop delivering the letters, and if you don't, I will pay you your due and you will never set foot inside this house again. And, believe me, I will make sure that all of Poitiers knows about it. No one, you hear me, no one will ever hire you."

Émilie Frasié pleaded that she was an old lady, that her daughter was dead and that she was raising her grandson alone, that she needed to work.

"If you want to stay, you will obey me, Frasié. It's either that or you're out. Period."

Émilie Frasié promised to do as she was told. She was sixty-one years old and needed to keep this job. Henriette Launier was pleased with herself. She had won. She asked the maid to play along with a deception, to go to the lawyer's house as usual but to tell him that Blanche wants nothing more to do with him, that it's over, and that Blanche has her eye on someone else. Obviously, they would not tell Blanche any of this, and all of the letters that she wrote to Gilles were to be given to Henriette Launier instead. Émilie agreed. She was in no position to refuse, as she needed the income from this job. If she were to be fired from this household, no one else would ever hire her, that was certain.

The next day, she went to Gilles Lomet's house and did as she was instructed. In her usual calm voice, she told the lawyer that Blanche never wanted to hear from him again.

Now that everything was settled with Émilie Frasié, Henriette Launier went to speak with her daughter. Once in her room, she proceeded straight to the hiding place and took out the letters. Blanche screamed for her to give them back.

"Understand me well, daughter, this whole thing is over. Over! You hear me?"

"I love him, and he loves me. We are going to get married, whether you like it or not. Give me back my letters!"

Henriette Launier would not hear of it. She went downstairs to the kitchen with Blanche on her heels furiously screaming for her letters back: "Those are mine!" Henriette charged past a frightened Céline Thébaud and threw the letters into the fire, shrieking: "It's over! Over, over, over! You are a bad girl, and you've betrayed my trust. You will burn in hell."

Céline, the cook, upset by this scene, looked on as Henriette turned her back to the fire that was consuming the last of the letters and Blanche sobbed to the point of convulsing.

"This man that you love does not love you back. He only wants our money."

"You're lying! You hate him. Well, I hate you! You hear me, I hate you!"

"If he were able to find a girl richer than you, he would marry her."

"I am going to marry Gilles, whether you and father agree or not."

"You will never marry that piece of trash. I can tell you that."

Blanche ran up to find her *grand-papa* and cried for hours in his arms, begging the whole time for him to intervene. Louis de Marcillat knew what his daughter could be like and knew that he had no hope of changing her mind, nor that of his son-in-law. He promised that he himself would deliver Blanche's letters to Gilles Lomet.

When Martin Launier got home from the Faculté des Lettres, Henriette filled him in on what was happening.

"If she ever married that Républicain," he said, "it would be the end of my career. I would never become dean of the college."

"If she ever married that man, we would have to move. And where would we go?"

One was concerned about money, the other about reputation and power. They were both in agreement. This marriage must never happen.

The next day, as promised, Louis de Marcillat got ready to go out; he put on a suit, picked up his dear Blanche's letter, and put it in his breast pocket. It had been several months since he had gone anywhere, so it was a surprise to Henriette when he appeared on the landing of the entryway stairs. Always suspicious, she inquired nervously: "Are you going to the cemetery?"

"It's none of your business."

"Would you like some company?"

"Mind your own business and let me go as I please."

He had a hard time getting down the stairs. Henriette tried to help and took his arm, but he pushed her aside forcefully. She was harming poor little Blanche, and he couldn't take it anymore. Also, it had been months since Henriette had even spoken to him. She never went up to visit him in his suite. Blanche was the only one who came to see him. His granddaughter was the only one who loved him, and she was suffering. As he pushed Henriette aside, he slipped and stumbled down a few steps.

They sent for an emergency doctor. Pierre Bauché arrived and diagnosed him as having a fractured femur. Louis de Marcillat was transported to the Hôtel-Dieu to get a cast put on.

In a month, Blanche would be twenty-five, only now there was no one to bring her letters to Gilles Lomet. Émilie Frasié insisted that Gilles did not want to hear from her, that he had his eye on another girl, and that she would no longer bring him letters that he didn't want.

Louis de Marcillat spent most of his time lying flat on the bed because of his leg. Soon he would need rehabilitation. He was not in any shape to go out. He hated having to call for assistance any time he needed to make the slightest movement. And not being able to help his granddaughter put him in a bad mood. He couldn't stand his daughter anymore. Whenever he had a little too much to drink, which happened more and more frequently, and he saw his daughter, he would threaten to revoke her power of attorney. So his daughter just avoided him and instructed the staff, Émilie Frasié in particular, not to argue with him. She also asked Céline Thébaud to prepare all of her father's favorite meals so as to keep him from complaining.

Blanche spent her time in her room with the curtains wide open, looking out onto the street, hoping to see Gilles. When she thought she saw him, she would throw the window open and wave her arms around, even though it was January and a very cold one at that. Marie Pinaud caught her doing this and informed her mother.

As soon as Martin Launier got home, Henriette pulled him aside to talk:

"Martin, our Blanche will turn twenty-five in nineteen days. We must do something to prevent this marriage. She spends all of her time at her window, and she might actually see Gilles one day."

"We could send her to my brother's house in Limoges."

"No, he'd have no authority over her. She'd just run off."

"How about we send her to Mont-de-Marsan, just until things settle down?"

"That would be just as bad. Honoré would never be able to control her."

"So, what should we do?"

"We need to keep her here and keep a close eye on her. We must do anything necessary to stop her from contacting that man. We should close the shutters on her window."

"How would we do that?"

"We'll call a carpenter, and he could nail them shut and put a padlock on them. That way, she won't be able to see who is walking by the house."

"But you know that will make people talk. The Lomet family will accuse us of holding her captive."

"Don't worry, I'll figure out a way to explain it. We must do this, I tell you, or all will be lost."

"And how will we explain this to the household staff?"

"I'll handle that. Let's call the carpenter, or we'll be out on the streets."

"If she were ever to marry that damned Républicain, it would be an absolute catastrophe."

"That lunatic is totally capable of helping her escape through the window. We must have those shutters permanently closed."

"If that's the only solution, then call for Justin Larot and let's be done with it."

That very day, Henriette Launier called for the carpenter to have him close the shutters on the window. While Blanche was in visiting with her grandfather,

Justin Larot placed a tall ladder on the side of the house, closed the shutters, nailed and locked them shut. On the inside, he crisscrossed two boards over the window and nailed them in place as well. Of course, he found it odd that he was being told to close up this window in such a permanent way, but he was being paid well, so he didn't ask questions and did what they wanted.

Henriette did pay him well, triple his normal fee. Justin Larot was Émilie Frasié's brother-in-law.

When Blanche got back to her room and saw that her shutters had been nailed shut, she grew very angry. She kept repeating: "My mother is insane, completely insane! She's keeping me locked up like an animal." In response, her mother noted that this was also her father's decision.

Blanche was beside herself. She tried to pry the shutters open, but had no luck. Then, she ran to her grandfather to tell him what happened. The old man listened without batting an eye and then asked Émilie Frasié to tell his daughter to come up.

"What's all this about shuttering up Blanche's window? You've lost your mind!"

"I am the one who will decide what is good for Blanche."

"You are going to open those shutters back up, and fast!"

"Don't get so upset. We closed up the shutters because we had to. Period."

Once Blanche had left and gone back to her room, Henriette returned to calm her father down. She explained that Blanche had started sleepwalking and that it was for her own good that the window was boarded up, so she wouldn't fall out. Her story was so convincing that the old man believed it.

That night, like many nights from then on, Blanche had an asthma attack. Her mother was wary of calling for a doctor, fearing that Blanche might tell him that her parents were holding her captive and show him the shuttered window. So, no doctor was called. When Pierre Bauché, the family doctor, came for lunch the next day as he normally did, Martin Launier told him about his daughter's asthma and asked what could be done. Dr. Bauché responded with a long-winded theoretical explanation, as if he were speaking with his medical school colleagues, and never once asked to see Blanche or bothered to find out if she had seen another doctor.

All that the Launiers retained from his lengthy erudite dissertation was this: during an asthma attack, you must force the person to sit upright so that they don't asphyxiate, even if it means tying them to the headboard of the bed. You could also dab their forehead with a damp cloth and try to reassure them. Dr. Bauché prescribed a calming potion that they could administer every night, a half-hour before bedtime. It was an ether-based sedative that Henriette Launier would use on Blanche and administer in excess.

For several days, Blanche refused to come downstairs to eat. Marie Pinaud would bring food up to her, but she wouldn't touch it. The sight of the shuttered window made her throat close up. Sometimes, she would eat a little bit when she was with her *grand-papa*, which was where she spent the vast majority of her time. She was waiting for him to get better and had put all of her hopes to ever see Gilles again into his recovery. She had said to her mother: "You can do whatever you want to me, but you cannot stop me from loving Gilles, nor him from loving me. We will get married one day. I promise you that."

Henriette Launier had always considered her daughter to be lacking in personality, but faced with her strong will, she began to fear the worst. From then on, the main door to the house was always locked, even during the day. Only the butler, her husband, and she herself had keys. Further, at night she would lock the doors to every single room on the ground floor where there was a window facing the street, just in case Blanche might think of escaping.

Émilie Frasié, the maid who spent the most time with Blanche, reported in regularly to Henriette. This is how she learned that even though Blanche was distraught, even though she had asthma attacks every night, even though she hated the shuttered window, she was in no way discouraged. As her mother feared, Blanche was steadfast in her conviction: she would not give up on Gilles Lomet.

As for Gilles Lomet, he was completely befuddled. He and Blanche had been in love for years and had promised to marry each other; just a few days ago, they were in each other's arms, and suddenly, out of the blue, she no longer wanted to hear from him? He started to be on the lookout for Émilie Frasié, and when he saw her in the street, he'd inquire about Blanche, but the maid was intractable. Blanche was going to marry another man and did not want to see him or receive letters from him anymore. Émilie would emphatically refuse to take any letters from Gilles.

Every day after court, Maître Gilles Lomet would return home by way of Rue de la Visitation, praying to God that he might see the woman he loved even more now that he couldn't be with her. He searched the house's windows, but never saw her. He did not know which room was Blanche's, so he looked at each window one by one, hoping for a miracle. He did notice that one window always had the shutters closed. From the street, you couldn't see that it was locked shut; he thought it might be the grandfather's chamber, knowing he had been keeping to his room ever since the death of his wife. It never crossed his mind that the shuttered window could be Blanche's room and that it had been hermetically sealed. After stopping in front of 21 Rue de la Visitation, heartbroken, he would tell the coachman to continue on home. He was as sad as could be. And he never noticed that, sometimes, on the sidewalk, directly beneath the shuttered window, there would be a stray envelope. Words of desperation that Blanche would launch through a crack, though no one ever noticed.

One morning, however, Marie Pinaud did see a letter fall down into the street. She picked it up and, good servant that she was, immediately delivered it to Henriette Launier. Furious, Henriette called the staff together and told them: "If you find a letter under my daughter's window, pick it up and bring it to me right away. Everything in those letters is false! Fabrications!"

What she had read in the letter Marie Pinaud brought her was this: "They are keeping me prisoner here. Please find Maître Gilles Lomet and tell him to come free me from this place!" Like bottles tossed into the sea, Blanche would fling these messages out of the window, complaining about imprisonment and cruel parents...

As expected, neighbors made comments about this window with the shutters always closed. Henriette Launier had an answer for everything: since her mother's death, her father had become quite unbalanced. He had started sleepwalking and could easily take a spill. He had already had a bad fall inside the house, so just imagine if he fell from the window. And then everyone praised the dutiful daughter who loved her father so much that she kept him home to care for him instead of sending him to a hospice.

Henriette Launier had instructed the household staff to give the same response if questioned. She made each one of them feel important, like keeping this secret for her was something that any high-class professional staff member was duty-bound to do, and if that wasn't enough, she also intimated that failure to do so would result in being released from employment. None of the staff wanted any trouble. They also knew who Blanche was in love with, and since no one in the house liked Républicains, they reassured themselves that Madame was only doing what needed to be done.

Right around then, two letters arrived from Mont-de-Marsan: one for Blanche and one for Monsieur and Madame Launier. As always, Henriette began by reading Blanche's letter first. She knew the letter was from her son, but it was always better to be extra cautious.

February 25, 1874

Dear little Sister,

Happy birthday! I'm sending you a small gift with this letter. I haven't written a lot lately because I met a young woman: Maria-Teresa de Pongère. I waited until I was sure how she felt about me, but I've been sure since the moment I first saw her. From the moment we met, I just knew that she would be the one for me. So, now you know. I've met my future wife, and I'm writing to tell you that we will be married in three months' time, assuming our parents approve. We would like to have the wedding on June 17, which is Maria-Teresa's grandmother's birthday. She really loves her grandmother.

I'm definitely counting on you. I know that you've been quite fatigued recently, but you have until June 17 to get better. You've never been to a wedding; I'm sure you'll have fun and maybe even meet your prince charming. That's my wish for you, as you're twenty-five now and it's time you got married. Most girls are already married by that age.

With love and affection,
Your brother Honoré

This letter was like a punch in the gut for Blanche. Her brother was to be married, but not her. Her brother was happy, while she was alone without any news from Gilles for over a month. She was at an impasse. It would be months before her grandfather would be able to walk again and transport her letters. And her brother had twisted the knife by adding that most girls of her age were already married. She knew full well. She wept as she read the letter and for some time afterwards. She loved her brother and would have confided in him. She had already written a letter to tell him everything, but as usual, her mother must have intercepted it or he wouldn't have gone on like that. Now she was sure, even her letters to Honoré were not getting out. They must have been tossed in the fire, like the others.

Blanche decided that she would not attend the wedding. She didn't have it in her to be cheerful or to dance. She would stay home, whether they liked it or not. That day, she felt more alone than ever before. In the afternoon, she scribbled the following on the wallpaper in her room: "Dear God, what did I do to deserve such monsters as parents? Have I forever lost my freedom?"

And she sat down to write a letter in dismay: "Oh, Gilles! I do love you. Do not forget me! Rescue me from their clutches!"

She gave the letter to Émilie Frasié, who accepted it with a smile, as if she were going to deliver it to Maître Lomet. But five minutes later, she gave it to Madame

Launier who became incensed again as she read it. Would this affair never end? She settled on yet another fabrication so that she might rid herself of this Lomet intruder once and for all.

"Maître Lomet is going to be married. He's engaged to Bernadette Crémieux." That's what everyone in the de Marcillat household was gossiping about. Émilie Frasié had mentioned it to the other maids, and the word had soon spread. Blanche heard it from her own mother's mouth: "Gilles Lomet is to be married."

Henriette Launier was determined to destroy her daughter's love for that lawyer. She insisted it was the truth, despite Blanche's visible suffering. The girl kept repeating *"Ce n'est pas vrai!"*; it can't be true! But she was worried because she was no longer receiving responses to her letters. Gilles was behaving as if she didn't exist, as if she no longer existed, as if there were someone else in his life.

"I told you so, daughter. That lawyer was not the right one for you. He found another girl who has more money, so he ditched you."

"If he wanted to break it off, he would have written to me. How do you explain the fact that he hasn't written to me?"

"Because he's a rat, like all Républicains are."

"In his last letter, he said that he loved me."

"And how long ago was that? Open your eyes. Get those silly childish thoughts out of your head. The wedding banns have been published. In two weeks, you will hear the church bells ring for them. That's just how it is."

Blanche was unhappy, but despite what everyone was saying, she still couldn't believe it. Her Gilles with another woman? In her heart, she knew it was false. So, she wrote a long letter to him, reminding him of their love and their promise to marry each other. She mentioned the rumors about Bernadette Crémieux, someone she only knew by name. According to her mother, Bernadette was one of the wealthiest girls in Poitiers.

It was Henriette Launier's idea to make Blanche believe that Gilles was engaged to another. She wanted to put an end to Blanche's feelings for him, to be rid of this specter threatening to ruin everything for her. Blanche was now twenty-five years old. If she were ever able to escape from their mansion, she could force her parents to accept this shameful union. Henriette Launier had taken the precaution of making sure that a wedding was going to occur at the Protestant church in two weeks, and it would be the final scene of the fiction she had invented. She simply had to make it seem real, and she was determined to do so!

On the Saturday that a wedding was to take place, Henriette Launier and her trusted maid Marie Pinaud, along with Stéphanie Parent, who was the strongest of the household staff, led Blanche to the street where the Protestant church was located. The maids were on either side of the girl, each holding one of Blanche's arms. They were close enough that you could see there was a wedding happening at the church, but far enough away that you couldn't tell exactly who the people were, particularly not who the bride and groom were. And they waited.

As Henriette had hoped, Blanche's imagination had been so primed for this event that she actually believed she saw Gilles, her Gilles, coming out of the church that day. Marie Pinaud and Stéphanie Parent guided her back to Rue de la Visitation, practically carrying her listless body, and as they arrived back home, she crumpled onto the floor.

That night, she had a terrible and unexplained fever that made her delirious. Émilie Frasié spent the whole night dabbing her forehead with a cool compress. Afterwards, for a full month, Blanche refused to eat, would only drink herbal tea, and never left her bed.

June 17, 1874

Martin and Henriette Launier, Blanche, Émilie Frasié, and Marie Pinaud left Poitiers two days before Honoré's wedding with three suitcases containing their best outfits. They arrived in Mont-de-Marsan the next morning, exhausted after having to change trains several times and wait for connecting trains that took forever to arrive. Louis de Marcillat remained at home, not wanting to leave his suite.

In the end, Blanche had gone with them, but it was against her will. There was no way her parents would leave her alone at 21 Rue de la Visitation, even if some of the staff were still there. For a full month, she hadn't left her bed, and for the month after that she spent most of her time there, explaining that she had no energy and that she thought she was dying. The mere idea of a wedding would make her weep. She mourned the wedding she would never have and was desolate deep down in her soul. The depression she had fallen into ever since the day she witnessed Gilles' wedding and heard those church bells ringing was so severe that it seemed nothing could pull her out of it.

Obviously, Blanche had not selected the clothes she would wear to her brother's wedding; her mother had done that. Delighted that her son was to marry an aristocrat, the granddaughter of a Spanish nobleman, Henriette Launier had made sure that at the very least Blanche's clothing would be worthy of this event. But she had chosen the outfits without looking at her daughter's face, and the greyish-pink outfit that she had picked for the voyage only accentuated Blanche's pallid skin and the dark circles under her eyes.

Nonetheless, Henriette Launier had gotten what she wanted: a son who made her proud. All of Poitiers knew about the marriage, for she had sent wedding announcements to everyone important in Poitiers' high society. And her daughter had finally given up on a love that was, in her eyes, unnatural. Although she was weak, Blanche was no longer causing trouble. With a blank stare, very rare movements, and an occasional stray tear that she would quickly wipe away, Blanche was going along with whatever she was told to do. She had arrived in Mont-de-Marsan with her hair done in a long braid off to one side and attended the wedding with a high bun that accentuated her thin face and was not very flattering.

All of the guests noticed the sad sister of the groom who could barely stand up and who refused all invitations to dance. Any potential suitor who tried to engage in conversation with her was quickly bored to death and excused himself as soon as he could think of a way to take his leave.

The day itself was magnificent. All of the elite society were there, and the food was abundant. There were Spanish dances along with the traditional French ones, followed by a grand cotillion. The parents and grandparents of the bride were as high class as they come, beautiful and majestic. Honoré had also gotten what he wanted: a wife to complement his official appointment. Like his mother, his wishes had been fulfilled, and he could now start to think about children.

Honoré's bride, Maria-Teresa, was a young woman who resembled his sister, back when she was in good health. She too had long black hair, but she had the beautiful round cheeks and the olive skin of someone who spent quite a bit of time outdoors. She was radiant, while poor Blanche only inspired pity from the guests who thought she must be suffering from some kind of neurosis.

Blanche barely ate anything. She mindlessly took one bite of the cake. This wedding was torture for her. All she wanted was to return to Poitiers and go back to her room. Her brother's happiness, the blissfulness of the bride in the beautiful white dress, the joy that filled the function hall at the Mont-de-Marsan prefecture... all of this pained her. Gilles had abandoned her, and now she would never marry.

Blanche returned from her brother's wedding more depressed than before. Remembering the promise that she had made to her grandmother, she forced herself to get out of bed every afternoon to go keep her grandfather company. The summer of 1874 was brutally hot. Even though she kept telling her mother that she was better and that the shutters could be opened, she appreciated how cool the room was now that no sunlight entered. The only other window, a small dormer window that opened onto the courtyard side of the house, rarely let in any light.

In the morning, she would stay stretched out on her bed remembering the happy times when her grandmother was alive, when Gilles still loved her, when her awful parents who had ruined her life were away in Paris, when she felt at peace. They used to go to the seashore this time of year or go out in a row boat on the Clain River. She remembered romantic summer evenings strolling by the river with Gilles, his arm around her waist.

She suddenly had the urge to go to La Rochelle again for a swim. She got out her bathing suit; it had stripes like a sailor's shirt and covered her down to her ankles. She felt her strength coming back and wanted to go out for a walk, with or without Gilles. She finally wanted to go out, to live again. So, she went to speak with her mother.

"*Maman*, let's go to the seashore with father and grandfather next Sunday!"

"To the seashore? But your father and I have never gone there."

"You'll see. It's fantastic. Please say yes!"

"How do you know it's so fantastic?"

"I went there with *grand-maman* and *grand-papa*."

"Without my permission?"

"*Maman*... grandfather loves to go to swimming. He adores fresh oysters."

"Our fishmonger has the freshest oysters in the region."

"Let's go to the coast, *maman*, you'll see. You'll like it."

"Just because everyone else does it, doesn't mean it's worth doing."

"But it's the thing to do. Everyone loves it."

"You want to go swimming with coachmen and farmhands and nursemaids? You want to mingle with those kinds of people. Is that it?"

"The coastline is huge. There's room for everyone."

"As frail as you are, you might fall ill."

"I feel better. Think about *grand-papa*. The salt water is good for his bones."

"If your grandfather desires a salt bath, he can have one here. But let's see what your father says about this."

At the dinner table, Blanche broached the idea again. Martin Launier sent a note to see if Pierre Bauché ever went to the seashore. Not getting a response, he asked about it the next time he saw the family doctor. It turned out that the director of the School of Medicine had never set foot in the ocean. Adrien de Fresnay had never gone to the beach either. In general, none of the white-haired gentlemen of Poitiers ever went there. Only young people went to swim at La Rochelle.

Martin Launier knew that the dean of the Faculté des Lettres would be retiring in six months. It was not a great time to draw attention to himself. He had just received a letter from the Duc de Landry. For now, he just had to lay low and wait. The position was practically his. This was not the time to take a trip to La Rochelle!

The idea of going swimming at the seashore was definitely a nonstarter.

∾

January 1875

Adrien de Fresnay never had the time to enjoy his retirement. He died, stupidly, after being hit by a horse-drawn carriage. Martin Launier replaced him sooner than expected as the head of the prestigious Faculté des Lettres. The pride that he and his wife felt that day was unparalleled. They had wanted this for years and had spent years plotting to make it happen, both in Paris and in Poitiers, years of patience that finally had come to fruition! They had been successful in ridding themselves of that lawyer, that Républicain whose name was never mentioned again by their daughter. They had it all.

They decided to host a reception that would be worthy of such an important appointment.

Henriette Launier again thought of everything. She invited all of the grey-haired power brokers in the city and all of Poitiers' wealthiest and most noble families. Only the adults were invited, of course. Henriette was convinced that young people would only spell trouble. She did not want her daughter to attend this event, fearing that some careless guest might let slip that Gilles Lomet was still single. She knew her daughter, and if ever she were to learn the truth, all hell would break loose. Once again, Henriette Launier made sure to keep the charade going. She convinced Blanche that this evening would be terribly boring and that it would be better for her if she didn't attend.

When she found out that her father had been named dean of the college, Blanche rejoiced. She had heard her parents say many times that the reason they refused to allow her to marry Gilles was because they had their sights set on this post for her father. But she did not resent them. Ever since Gilles had betrayed her, had made it clear that he was not worthy of her, she had slowly grown closer to her parents. In particular, she had developed a relationship with her father, who often agreed to take her out for walks in Blossac Park. Her mother obstinately refused any outing other than mass, vespers, and confessions at church.

Henriette was successful in keeping her daughter from attending this memorable soirée. With the same shrewdness, she continued to insist on personally receiving all of the mail from the postman so that she could remove any letters addressed to Blanche. There may be invitations from other young women to attend a ball or an engagement party or even a wedding. She still worried that Blanche might somehow ruin her husband's career, or her son's for that matter, since he aspired to be named prefect of Poitiers. It had always been his goal. So, she continued to keep Blanche in the dark.

When her grandmother was alive, Blanche used to get all kinds of social invitations, and she was surprised that she no longer received any mail at all. In particular, she had never received any responses after sending several letters to her dearest and best friend. She had given the letters to her mother to post, but in reality, they ended up in the woodstove.

Henriette Launier was so guarded about her daughter that she ended up getting mad at Blanche's godmother, who was the wife of the former principal of the Royal Academy. She used to come over once a week, and she had a daughter Blanche's age. She was surprised that Blanche never came down to see her when she was visiting, as Henriette always made some excuse about Blanche being too tired. So, she suggested that her daughter come along to spend the afternoon with Blanche and keep her company. Henriette categorically refused and was unable to hide her irritation. The next week, when the godmother arrived at 21 Rue de la Visitation, no one opened the door. She would never be invited over to Henriette Launier's house again.

At the Faculté des Lettres, in an amphitheater filled with eager literature students, surrounded by all of the distinguished professors, Martin Launier gave a speech that everyone applauded. He spoke of the illustrious history of the institution and of all its previous deans. Afterwards, they all walked over to the library for liqueurs and petits fours, a reception organized by the General Secretary. There were reporters in attendance from all of the best regional newspapers.

His speech was reprinted in entirety in the newspapers. He had been nominated to this post thanks to his good friend the Duc de Landry, and he was going to make sure everyone was aware of it. He had worked for the Emperor, he reminded them, and repeatedly mentioned his Royalist convictions. Martin Launier was on top of the world. In Paris, as in the rest of the country, the Royalists were in power. He had been speaking to Royalist professors, and he gave a press conference that followed suit:

"The Empire and the aristocracy are the ones who built this country. The nation owes them. Men of proven valor are in control now. Today's youth hear speeches attacking the concept of morality, and fears of moral decay spread, but I, Martin Launier, Dean of the Faculté des Lettres, I intend to hold the bar high. For only morality and order will keep our country prosperous. For this, we need teachers who believe that moral order is essential to our stability. It is the teachers who are shaping the minds of tomorrow's elite society. Their instruction must take into account the fundamental facts necessary to build the society of tomorrow. From the prestigious high post that I now occupy, I assure you this will be my priority, just as it was for my predecessors. I will keep watch over our youth, just as others kept watch over me. We will show them the right path. *Vive la Faculté! Vive la France!*"

⌒

Poitiers, January 6, 1875

To my dear friend the Duc de Landry,

My first words for you are: "merci beaucoup!" Thank you again and from the bottom of my heart for having nominated me to become dean of the Faculté des Lettres, this college I cherish so very much. Never fear, I will put all of my talent and all of my energy in to keeping it as glorious as it has always been. The new dean of Poitiers is forever grateful to you.

How are you? How is your arthritis doing with the damp air this season? I spoke to Pierre Bauché about your condition; he is the director of the School of Medicine. He suggested that you might try Orezza water. It's an excellent sparkling mineral water that is rich in iron. It's the best one and is perfectly pure.

With a slightly acidic flavor, rather sharp, it is even quite enjoyable to drink.

How is your lovely wife? Please send her my best. Before spring, I intend to make a quick trip to Paris and will wish her well in person.

I would like to ask you for one more favor, not for me as I have everything I could have ever wished for, but for my son. You had him appointed as counsel to the prefecture in Mont-de-Marsan. Well, I've learned from the Marquis de Chauvigny that Chabot, the subprefect of Puget-Théniers in the Alpes-Maritimes region, is about to retire. He's almost sixty-two years old!

My son now has experience working in a prefecture and, as you know, brilliantly defended his thesis in law. He is, in my mind, the ideal candidate for this post as he waits to become prefect of Poitiers. For him to advance in this career, he shouldn't stay for too long as counsel to the prefecture.

It goes without saying that Honoré is as devoted to our cause as I am and my new daughter-in-law, descended from Spanish nobility, is of the same mind and knows how to uphold our values. When the time comes, both of them will be an excellent infusion of new blood in this region where Républicains have such a strong base.

Respectfully yours,
Martin Launier

It really was great to be friends with the Duc de Landry. Exactly twelve days later, Honoré Launier and his wife left Mont-de-Marsan for a stay in Poitiers before moving to Puget-Théniers. The following week, Honoré became subprefect of that city. He was only twenty-seven years old. Théodore Chabot had unexpectedly been asked to retire and did so, even though it was not at all what he had planned to do.

Martin Launier was happy about his son's nomination, but it was not a surprise. He had been expecting it. He knew the Duc de Landry really well. Their friendship was solid, having lasted through many difficult situations, and their shared political opinions made their bond even stronger. He never doubted for a moment whether the Duc would intervene on behalf of his son.

Henriette Launier was relieved to hear of her son's nomination. She had, of course, read the letter that her husband had sent to the Duc de Landry, but until the nomination was finalized, she still feared that it might not happen. She was worried that the Duc might get tired of their requests for favors or that it might be refused for some other unknown reason. When she finally heard the good news, she had such a rush of pride that she almost fainted. She went to the train station in Poitiers to greet her son and daughter-in-law and brought along the entire staff to transport their luggage to the house.

Blanche was glad to hear of her brother's promotion, but happier still to see him again. She was counting on him to ease the ongoing tension with her mother and to intervene on her behalf so that she might be allowed to go out on her own again, as she did when her grandmother was alive, and above all so that her shutters might be opened up again.

When her brother arrived, she threw her arms around him and also gave Maria-Teresa a big hug. Just seeing their faces made her feel better, like her strength was coming back. Honoré thought she looked beautiful, even if she was much too thin.

For the two full days they were in Poitiers, Honoré and his wife did not have a moment alone. Henriette and Martin Launier wanted to show off their subprefect son to everyone they knew. It was one gathering after another and plenty of congratulatory visits, though Blanche mostly declined to attend.

When it came time for the young couple to leave for Puget-Théniers, Honoré pulled his mother aside to ask permission to bring Blanche with him for a few weeks so that she might benefit from the clean mountain air. Henriette Launier categorically refused, saying that her husband would never agree to it and that it was better not to upset him.

The truth was that she trusted no one and had as little faith in her son as she did in her daughter. Even though neither mother nor daughter ever spoke of Gilles Lomet anymore, Henriette Launier had been so terrorized by him and his family that she always remained wary of their love somehow being rekindled.

The Royalists were in power at that time, so Martin Launier was at peace. He was unaware of all of the deals and negotiations happening in Paris. He was a man who was set in his ways. He had been appointed dean of the college thanks to his fidelity to the monarchy, and he was steadfast in his beliefs. From the start of his tenure as dean, he began to make enemies. The fact that a new mayor had been elected in Poitiers—a Républicain—had no impact on the power of the noble families in the region. But it should have given Martin Launier pause.

In national politics, the internal squabbling among Royalist factions was leading to a consensus about establishing a monarchy with limited powers; but, in fact, the political future of France was still very much unsettled in the early part of the year 1875.

The National Assembly, with a Royalist majority, was voting on constitutional laws. Amidst all of their debates, a moderate named Henri Wallon introduced an amendment on January 30 proposing that a president of the "Republic" be elected for a seven-year term. His amendment passed by one vote, 353 for and 352 against, definitively establishing the Third Republic and earning him a place in the history books.

From February to November, elected officials of the National Assembly approved three more constitutional laws to regulate the Senate, public authorities, and the relationship between these two entities. Thanks to these laws, there was to be an election to choose a President of the Republic who would serve for seven years. The country would also elect congressmen to serve four-year terms in the Chamber of Deputies, which was granted legislative power. The Senate would be comprised of both "members for life" and those elected by municipalities. In Paris, a new Republic was being formed.

The Royalist majority had created a system that was flexible enough to allow for the establishment of a constitutional monarchy, should that day ever arrive. The man elected to be President of the Republic was a Royalist, Patrice de MacMahon. It was indeed a republic, but one led by Royalists, a tour de force by the conservatives!

Far from Paris, Martin Launier was quite content, for he had every reason to be. When he looked back on his life, he realized how far he had come from being the son of a humble hairdresser in a small town. His father had put all of his hopes in him. First, he was sent to a private Catholic school, then to the Faculté des Lettres. After earning a university diploma, he became a teacher at the Royal Academy in Poitiers, then married into a wealthy aristocratic family. Thanks to his mother-in-law's connections, he had been named private tutor to the Emperor's son. Then, he completed his doctoral thesis, which was a brilliant success, became a professor at the Faculté des Lettres and was soon promoted to become the dean of the college!

He had studied the careers of his predecessors and knew that once you became dean, it was your post until you chose to retire. He had many years to go, for he was a young appointee at age fifty-five. He was determined to be a dynamic dean. He loved everything about this college, his college. He loved it for what it was and what it had always been: a place to educate the nation's elite. He would make sure that no pesky Républicains would infect his student body. He would give firm orders that such troublemakers be detected in their first year so that they could be dismissed before doing any harm. Any kind of disorder was to be nipped in the bud...the Faculté des Lettres was not a place for debate. Anyone wishing to engage in political activism should go elsewhere!

Every day, Martin Launier read two newspapers: *Le Courrier de la Vienne et des Deux-Sèvres*, a Royalist paper, and *Le Journal de l'Ouest*, a Bonapartist one. This is how he learned about what was happening in Paris at the National Assembly. France had become a republic again, but how long would that last? During his lifetime, he had seen so many regime changes that this one didn't worry him too much. Furthermore, the articles he was reading were quite clear about one thing: the way that the constitutional laws were written allowed for the possibility of having a king as head of state rather than a president. A modern monarchy, like the one in England, that's what France needed. For Royalists, all was not lost. In truth, they were still controlling the country with MacMahon, a well-known Royalist, as President of the Republic and a large Royalist majority in the National Assembly.

The anarchist attacks had hurt the Républicains, and they had not yet recovered from that hit. Most French people favored tradition and stability and wanted their government officials to be good Catholics. Martin Launier had confidence that all would be well. He spent his days with the professors in his college, and all of them were Royalists. He could not imagine that there might be university professors anywhere in France who weren't Royalists.

At home, Martin had become a pleasant and charming man. He had completely forgotten about the lawyer, Gilles Lomet. His relationship with Blanche was improving. He allowed his wife to continue to enforce her rule that Blanche not be allowed to go out alone, but on Sundays, he often took his daughter with him to the land they owned in the countryside. There, they would go fishing or go for long walks or ride horses, and Blanche's health began to improve. She started to gain some weight and the color came back to her cheeks.

These outings helped Blanche to survive being locked up in the house and constantly surveilled by her mother. Her mother's iron rule was oppressive, heavy, smothering, and permanent, for she also had a powerful grip on her father.

Martin thought it might be time to find a suitable husband for Blanche, a Royalist. Henriette would not hear of it, arguing that she didn't see the point and, anyway, that Blanche was so fragile that a pregnancy might actually endanger her life. In reality, the idea of providing a dowry for her daughter and risking the loss of her fortune made her sick to her stomach.

～

1876–1877

Adolphe Thiers had been a politician with divided loyalties, equally sympathetic to both the Royalist and Républicain causes. He died on September 3, 1877 in Saint-Germain-en-Laye, and with him vanished a generation of people who could not make up their minds.

During the legislative elections of 1876, Républicains took over the majority of elected seats, so the new Prime Minister had to be chosen from their party. The Royalist president, MacMahon, was forced to hand over power to a Républicain. He chose Jules Armand Dufaure, but was not satisfied with his leadership and quickly replaced him with Jules Simon.

Jules Simon was in favor of schools to support the Republic, and for that they needed deans who were Républicains. In Poitiers, Gilles Lomet had heard the complaints of students at the Faculté des Lettres who were Républicains. They explained how the dean, Martin Launier, singled them out for dismissal in their first year. Maître Lomet wrote to Jules Simon to demand the dean's removal. Martin Launier did not see it coming and lost his post. The new dean of the Faculté des Lettres in Poitiers was even younger. A supporter of the Republic, he decided that he should also clean house, this time dismissing any students who espoused Royalist views.

In May 1877, President MacMahon had a conflict of opinion with Jules Simon and fired him. He appointed a Royalist, the Duc de Broglie, as Prime Minister. There was an uproar in the Chamber of Deputies. MacMahon did not back down and dissolved the National Assembly. He was backed by the Senate, which was majority Royalist. The summer of 1877 was consumed by an electoral battle. In Poitiers, as in other cities, the campaigning was fierce. Maître Jacob Lomet, Gilles' father, decided to run again, this time with his son there to advocate for him. Martin Launier naturally supported the Marquis de Chauvigny, a Royalist who was almost seventy years old. And something that had never happened before finally occurred: Gilles Lomet went head-to-head with Martin Launier in a political debate.

The lawyer, who was still in love with Blanche, wanted revenge for being refused her hand in marriage. It was because of the Launiers that he and Blanche could not be together. Gilles Lomet showed no pity, taking the opposite side and countering every argument Martin Launier tried to make. As wound up as ever, Henriette Launier pressed her husband to continue on.

But the Launiers could not stop the Républicains from victory in October of 1877; they won a large majority throughout France. Jacob Lomet won his election. It was clear that the country had set aside the anarchist attacks of the past and desired a true republic, one with Républicains in charge. Under pressure from the public, President MacMahon reinstated Dufaure as head of the cabinet, and he in turn surrounded himself with Républicains.

Two years later, there would be a shift in the Senate as well, as Républicains gained control there too. It was the end of the line for the Royalists.

Martin Launier was no longer dean of the college. He was still holding out hope for a new appointment, although he had fallen into such disgrace that they wouldn't even let him return as a professor at the Faculté des Lettres. It was a complete failure, and he could no longer count on the Duc de Landry, as his friend had lost all of his political clout. He continued his political activities, more Royalist than ever, as he was convinced that the Royalists would come back into power one day. He also doubled down on his belief in the moral order.

After the 1877 elections, Honoré was also removed from his post as subprefect in Puget-Théniers. He returned to Poitiers with his wife and took the only job available as counsel to the prefecture in Poitiers. As one might imagine, the mood in the de Marcillat household at that time was quite somber. The fact that Honoré had moved to Poitiers, just two streets over from his parents, was of no help to Blanche. She still could only go out in the company of her mother or father. Her brother and his wife would often come for lunch on Sundays at Rue de la Visitation, but since Blanche and her brother were not that close, she didn't think she could confide in him.

Sunday lunches after the high mass at the cathedral were not just for family. There were always guests, such as Dr. Bauché, a regular whom Henriette Launier favored, and other politicians and aristocrats like the Marquis de Chauvigny, who was still gunning to over-turn of the republic. During these meals, they would continually disparage the Républicains. This caused

Honoré Launier to limit his Sunday visits. As a government employee, he couldn't risk losing his job. He found his parents' political views to be quite extreme. Honoré had nothing against Républicains, and he just wanted to be left alone to restart his career.

One Sunday in April 1878, the topic of conversation turned away from politics and towards business. All anyone could talk about was the Panama Canal. The Marquis de Chauvigny told anyone who would listen that it was sure to be successful and that if you were smart, you would invest in the project.

Ferdinand de Lesseps, who had overseen work on the Suez Canal and had experience in this area, was taking on a new challenge. All of France supported him. The only problem was that he needed 600 million francs in order to complete the project. The big banks had dug in their heels, so the famous engineer had decided to appeal to the general public, in particular to private investors.

Financiers Cornelius Herz and the Baron de Reinach were in charge of raising the capital.

"This canal will create a link between the Atlantic and Pacific oceans."

"It will be eighty kilometers long and twelve meters deep!"

"There will be millions of tons of cargo passing through there... Cargo ships full of gold and diamonds."

"Even the Japanese will use this canal."

"It's the financial opportunity of the century!"

National and local newspapers praised the ingenuity of the project. The Marquis de Chauvigny made it known that he himself had invested all of his savings in the project. That day, Martin Launier finished his meal remarking that, indeed, one should not let such an incredible opportunity pass by. All of the guests agreed. The only person who did not agree was Henriette Launier, but she stayed silent on the issue. Any kind of investment was wasteful in her mind. She loved nothing more than to keep her gold locked up in a chest in her room.

∽

January 1879

MacMahon, the Royalist president, was still the head of state in France, and that gave Martin Launier reason to hope; but this Royalist President of the Republic was seventy-one years old and was starting to feel that he had served his time in office. He had had a long and fulfilling military and political career, having served during the French conquest of Algeria in the 1830s and 1840s and the campaign in Crimea in the 1850s. He then served under Napoléon III, winning a military victory for him in Magenta, Italy in 1859. The Emperor had rewarded him by naming him Maréchal de France and Duc de Magenta. Although he had been unlucky in Sedan during the Franco-Prussian war, he later led the French army that crushed the Paris Commune government. He was tired of being in power and submitted his resignation on January 30, 1879. In doing so, he left the Republic in the hands of the Républicains. There was a collective sigh of relief from Républicains across the nation, while in the Launier household it was more like a sad grumble.

MacMahon was replaced by Jules Grévy, a lawyer from the Jura region who was a moderate Républicain. He received 563 votes out of 713. All of the Républicain representatives voted for him, but some of the Royalists did too. One old man replaced another, as Grévy was seventy-two years old when he took office.

Jules Grévy wasted no time, and by 1880 had appointed the formidable Jules Ferry as Prime Minister. Ferry's time in power would alter the political landscape and influence public opinion in important ways. More than ever, the Royalists were bent on defending the public role of the Catholic Church, while Jules Ferry imagined a government that bowed to neither king nor God. He wanted to create a secular public school system, and his first order of business was to disband three hundred Catholic schools.

From Lille to Marseille, and certainly in Poitiers, Royalists protested this change. From that moment on, schooling would become Martin and Henriette Launier's *cause célèbre*, adding a new dimension to their longstanding campaign against the Républicains. They doubled down on defending the moral order.

Though his actions were brutal, Jules Ferry was a refined politician. He was aware that this new policy would shock both Royalists and Catholic Républicains, so he proposed a new law that stipulated that public primary school education would be not only secular but also free and compulsory. He knew that this would sway public opinion in his favor because many children did not have access to schooling and illiteracy was rampant.

In Poitiers, this caused the divide between Royalists and Républicains to continue to grow. Banquets were organized on both sides to explain what was at stake. The Launier family were staunch supporters of a traditional Catholic education, while the Lomet family championed the idea of an education system that was secular, free, and compulsory. Gilles Lomet, in particular, was an ardent defender of Jules Ferry's policies. When Gilles was a boy, there were no Protestant schools, so for years he attended a Catholic school where they forced him to pray for the Catholic Pope. He wanted to see a world where Protestant children could go to school without being required to study Catholic doctrine. He wrote about this issue regularly in the local newspapers and got the attention of local Protestants.

Likewise, Martin Launier voiced his conservative opinions in the Royalist newspapers. And he never missed a chance to badmouth the Lomets when entertaining at Rue de la Visitation. Their names were mentioned at virtually every meal.

"Those Républicains, the Lomets, they won't stop until they have killed all of the Catholics."

"Those Protestants are trying to rid our schools of all trace of God. They're monsters!"

"Tell me who is restarting the religious wars? Who?"

Blanche always listened but said nothing.

Jules Ferry did not stop there, continuing to propose laws that made the Launier family cringe. From 1883 to 1885, there was a law permitting the creation of associations among private citizens—Royalists saw this as allowing secret societies to exist—and a law legalizing divorce. They were sure this meant an end to the traditional family; it was organized chaos. For Royalists, French society was crumbling. For Gilles Lomet, the word "secular" meant political and religious neutrality, while for Martin Launier and his wife, it meant unleashing the devil and complete debauchery.

Jules Ferry, who knew he was on shaky ground, created what were called the *"écoles normales,"* schools to educate future teachers. They were separated by gender, with the school for men in Saint-Cloud and the school for women in Fontenay-aux-Roses. In the national curriculum, he included courses on morality, civics, and hygiene, which had never before been taught in schools. This tempered the fears of many who were leery of sweeping changes in the education system.

In March 1882, Martin Launier started to go to confession at the cathedral every Saturday. He used to go every other week. Many people suspected that he was going more regularly just to become more visible among the congregation, as he used to do during election campaigns, but that was not really his reason. The truth was that he was simply tired and was starting to worry about dying.

In the beginning of April, he became bedridden. His friend Dr. Bauché came to see him every day. He wasn't in the best of health either. He had arthritis, which caused discomfort and made it difficult for him to walk. He dragged his feet, and since it was hard for him to climb the stairs, a maid had to assist him up to Martin Launier's room.

The doctor found his friend to be thin, jaundiced, and fatigued, looking like he had not long to live. In moments of silence, he would nod his head solemnly. He prescribed a regimen that would allow his friend to die happy: a small cognac around ten o'clock in the morning, a glass of white wine at noon, a good red wine at five o'clock, and a hot rum toddy just before bed. He would spend hours at his friend's bedside and felt the need for deep conversations. They told each other everything they never before dared to say, making the most they had of these last days or maybe even last hours together.

One day, they changed the topic of conversation, veering away from their usual political discussions. They spoke about their lives, their respective children. Martin Launier talked about his son at length, wondering what he should do to climb the ranks at the prefecture. He worried, even saying it out loud, that his son might never make it. They also talked about Blanche.

"Is she still suffering from asthma attacks?"

"Less frequently now, but yes."

"You should think about finding her a husband. If she were settled, she wouldn't be having these attacks."

As usual, Martin Launier felt ill at ease, maybe even a little guilty, when talking about his daughter. He could sense the disapproval in his friend's voice. Sure, there were many who would marry Blanche, but why should she get married? She was thirty-three now and had everything she could possibly need. Why would she want to leave? Why give her to a man who didn't know anything about her? Who wouldn't be able to help when she had asthma attacks? No one could care for her better than he and his wife. No, he thought, not all girls need to marry; some are quite happy to stay close to their parents. He didn't say this out loud, though, for fear that he might be taken for an egotistical old geezer. Sure, people might think he was crazy, but his only concern was for his daughter's happiness. And who knew her better than he did?

One day, he felt the need to speak to his priest. So, Marie Pinaud went to fetch Father Mallouet at Saint-Porchaire Church. The priest had anticipated the real reason for the visit and brought with him an altar boy. He arrived in his surplice, with the Holy Communion. Father Mallouet had guessed right. Martin Launier wanted to receive his last rites, the final Catholic sacrament before death.

Father Mallouet was also quite elderly. He spent a long time hearing Martin Launier's final confession, while the altar boy paced back and forth in the hallway. After the last rites were administered, he sat with Martin for a while, chatting about this and that. Once again, the subject of children came up, and more questions about Blanche.

"How is the child doing?"

"She's doing fine."

"How is her asthma?"

"She still has it."

"You should find her a husband, while there's still time."

"She's happy here with us."

"It's not good for her to stay here and not bear children. God wants women to have children. If not, they fall ill. This may be the source of Blanche's illness."

"You're not a doctor."

"You're not immortal, and neither is your wife. Let me handle it. I know a woman who will be able to find her a good match."

"No, no, Father! It's out of the question."

Father Mallouet did not insist, vowing to try again one day with Henriette Launier. He had given last rites to many sick people in his time, and he knew what a dying man looked like. He gave Martin Launier no more than a week to live. After his burial, he thought to himself, I'll see to it that the girl is married. I've already waited too long to intervene.

Father Mallouet was correct about Martin Launier being on his deathbed, but he got one thing wrong. It all happened faster than expected. In fact, Martin Launier died that night, while explaining to his wife how he had been harassed by Dr. Bauché and Father Mallouet who had each insisted that Blanche should be married. He became so agitated the he almost choked to death. He didn't choke, though, he just died.

Martin Launier left this earth at the age of sixty-two. He was laid out in his room for two days, and there was an uninterrupted chain of political figures who came to pay their last respects. Even the Duc de Landry had come down from Paris. Henriette Launier did not write the announcement herself; she entrusted that task to Honoré. She advised him, however, to invite all of the Royalists in Poitiers and throughout the region to attend the funeral. The best printer in town was hired to design the invitations.

The burial took place on a freezing cold morning. A few snowflakes were falling from the sky. More than a thousand people had responded to Honoré Launier's invitation. The pile of flower bouquets was as large as the crowd. Royalists were not ungrateful people. They recognized that Martin Launier had faithfully served their cause, even though he hadn't been born to a noble family. This event was the last big Royalist gathering held in Poitiers. Martin Launier's death felt like the end of an era, and the Marquis de Chauvigny quietly wept at the ceremony. In a sense, people were right. Everything would be different from then on.

Louis de Marcillat refused to attend his son-in-law's funeral, on the pretext that he didn't feel up to it. He had never forgiven Martin for opposing the marriage of

Blanche and Gilles Lomet. As for the shuttered window, he couldn't bear to think of it, but he felt helpless in that household. Blanche confided in him, and only in him, so he knew that she was still upset about losing Gilles. Knowing that she was in so much pain, alone, unmarried, with no hope for the future made him an unhappy old man. He knew things would only get worse now that Martin was gone and his daughter had full control of everything. He knew how things would go. No, he would not attend the burial. His daughter and her husband were horrible people, thirsty for power. He had learned to live without them. He didn't even pay his last respects in the room where the body was laid out.

Martin Launier's funeral was in the cathedral. The bishop, Paul Duillaume, gave the homily, which lasted two hours. He was a fervent Royalist and made it known that day. His homily was so impactful that many people began to cry. Henriette made sure that there was a white flag hanging in the nave of the cathedral, near the flowers. Others had the same idea. There were several white flags in the crowd, one held by the Marquis de Chauvigny's assistant. It was a beautiful funeral. After the bell tolled, the hearse headed towards the cemetery, with everyone following behind on foot, which was a rare occurrence. The coaches that had been parked by the church followed far behind the parade of people. This is how Poitiers' nobility demonstrated how much Martin Launier would be missed.

Henriette Launier had prepared for this day. She had rented a hall, and a lovely meal had been prepared for all of these important people. The room held four hundred people, but many of the funeral attendees had to wait outside. The room was that packed. People were standing up, shoulder to shoulder, talking about the deceased or about politics. They spoke bitterly about recent events, speculating about how Jules Ferry's laws had killed Martin Launier. How far would Jules Ferry go? Where would that unholy man stop?

Just after her father had passed away, Blanche looked at him, finding him handsome and serene, as if he were sleeping. She was not upset about his death at that moment and didn't even cry at all, which incited her mother to call her an ingrate. It didn't register with Blanche that he was really gone until they lowered the casket into the ground. That's when her tears began to flow as she remembered the rare moments of happiness they had shared, walking in the countryside and fishing in the Clain River.

After the burial, she did not return to Rue de la Visitation. Accompanied by Marie Pinaud, she went in the family carriage to the reception hall. She was sad, but not as despondent as when her grandmother had died. She nibbled at her food. In the crowd, she found her best friend who told Blanche that she was married and had three children. The friend mentioned how upset she was that Blanche had refused to be her maid of honor and had not even attended her wedding. Surprised, Blanche explained that she didn't know anything about it and that she had never received any invitation to the wedding. Once the misunderstanding was cleared up, they spent the evening talking about the good old days. The two were so happy to be together again that they talked for hours on end, right up until it was time to go home.

Later, Blanche thought about what her friend had said and wondered if she were telling the truth. She even asked her mother about it, but her mother insisted that she had never received any mail or any invitation to the wedding. She blamed the postman for the missing letters.

VI

Henriette Launier had allowed her son to make all of the funeral arrangements because she just couldn't think about it. She had only one thing on her mind: the possibility that her children might put her out on the street and claim their share of the inheritance. Honoré and Blanche had the right to request an inventory of their father's assets, to sell the countryside property out in Pilet and to demand their share of the profit. Henriette Launier could not allow that to happen.

So, she paid a visit to Maître Billedoux and had a long conversation with him. The next day, he came to see her and her son Honoré at Rue de la Visitation. He explained things in a way that made his elderly client happy.

"You and your sister will each inherit a share of your father's assets."

"How much would that be?" asked Honoré.

"I'm not sure yet. We'll need to do an inventory."

"My son, an inventory is quite expensive," explained Henriette, "We don't really need one."

"Of course," the lawyer agreed, "you don't have to do one. Your mother would like to give you a generous monthly allowance, with only a few minor stipulations."

"How much would the allowance be?"

"Six hundred francs a month. It's a good number, right my son?"

"How is six hundred francs a good number? I have a wife and a daughter. You're not serious with this offer."

"How about a thousand?" the lawyer proposed, as Henriette rolled her eyes.

"Mother, I will accept two thousand francs or nothing at all."

"Two thousand francs?" Henriette wailed, "Do you want me to be destitute?"

"Take it or leave it," Honoré said with confidence, "Give me an allowance of two thousand francs a month, or I will demand my full inheritance now. That's the deal."

Henriette Launier slumped down, her shoulders hunched, her eyes fixed on the floor.

"What do you say, Madame?" The lawyer inquired.

"My own son is strangling me. What can I do?"

"Accept his deal!"

"I want this all in writing," added Honoré, "I will not take your word for it."

And so, Henriette Launier, with tears in her eyes, agreed to sign off on giving her son Honoré an allowance of two thousand francs a month. Not wanting to have the same discussion with her daughter, whom she feared might be ill advised by her *grand-papa*, Henriette paid a second visit to Maître Billedoux's office. She had a different plan for Blanche, she said, since her son had just bled her dry. In the end, she was able to convince him that Blanche should not receive the same allowance.

"My daughter will not be at a disadvantage. You see, I take care of all of Blanche's needs."

"She's not a minor anymore. She may want to have a life of her own."

"My little girl...she wants nothing more than to stay home with her *maman*. It's the only home she's ever known, and she's happy there."

"She's old enough to get married."

"She likes staying home with me."

"She might change her mind."

"If she does, we'll reconsider. Anyway, the house is big enough. A young couple could easily live there with me."

"The best thing to do would be to give her an allowance, like her brother."

"But Maître Billedoux, an allowance only goes so far. I give her everything, everything she asks for. In my home, she can have all that she desires, every day."

"My worry is that if there is no allowance, it may look like you are taking advantage of her."

"Very well, I'll give her an allowance, but I'll take care of it privately. I don't want to sign any papers to make it official. I'll just give her money whenever she asks for it. If there are contracts involved, it will just cause a problem with her brother. I give my little Blanche so much. I don't want her brother to sue me for more money. You saw how greedy he was."

"So, to avoid a conflict, you want to make this a verbal agreement with Blanche."

"Correct, yes, a verbal agreement."

"But you will keep your word."

"You've known me for so long, and you know that I am an honorable woman. But, between us, let's not state a fixed amount. I give her so much more than what is due."

That day, Maître Billedoux met with Blanche and her mother. After a short speech that made little sense to Blanche but that had something to do with her best interests, he asked her to sign a paper that would allow her mother to manage all of the assets from her inheritance.

Martin Launier's funeral had been a splendid show of Royalist pageantry, but it was not without consequence. Less than a month later, Honoré Launier was called to the office of the prefect of Poitiers and informed quite plainly that he was no longer counsel to the prefecture, but now just a secretary.

It was not difficult for Honoré to come to the conclusion that his demotion was the result of the incredible Royalist spectacle that was his father's funeral. He would remain angry at his mother for quite some time after that. In a tizzy, he charged over to share the news with her.

"Well, you've won!"

"Won what? Why are you so agitated? Why are you yelling?"

"I'm no longer counsel to the prefecture."

"So, what are you then?"

"I'm nothing, nothing at all. Thanks to your ridiculous pride, I will never be subprefect."

"Who told you that?"

"The prefect of Poitiers. From now on, I'm nothing but an errand boy at the prefecture. I wasn't fired, but I might as well have been. Do you understand?"

Henriette Launier turned pale: "Another low blow from that Lomet family!"

"Leave the Lomet family out of this. It's your fault and yours alone. Why did you have to invite all of those dukes and marquis? Are those the only people who matter to you?"

"Your father would never have become dean of the Faculté des Lettres without those people whom you seem to despise. Have you forgotten that?"

"Times have changed, Mother. The Royalists are no longer in power. They're done. Don't you understand? I've been demoted. I'm just lucky I wasn't fired."

"You of all people, with all of your degrees, should know that no political situation is irreversible."

"*Bon sang*, when will you realize that this country is now Républicain. The prefect is a Républicain. France is a Republic!"

"Republics never last for long. They've never lasted forever, and they won't last forever."

"I cannot comprehend your stubbornness. I really hope that when grandfather dies you won't make me invite all of the aristocrats in the country to his funeral. If you ever try to do that, I will demand double my monthly allowance because I will be out of work. Do you hear me, mother? I have a wife and a daughter to feed."

"Lower your voice! You will not tell me what to do."

"My name is Honoré Launier. My father's father was a hairdresser. *Grand-papa* worked at the stock exchange. I earned my diplomas through hard work. I am not a duke or a marquis. I just need to live."

The fact that her son had been demoted to the position of secretary in the prefecture, in the prefecture of Poitiers, her city! Henriette Launier considered this to be the ultimate disgrace. For days, she did not go out in public. At home, she was unbearable, shouting loudly that the Lomet family would pay for this insult. She didn't know how just yet, but she would think of something.

That said, she would not dare to miss Sunday mass. When she returned, filled with shame and convinced that everyone had seen her and gossiped about her family, she took it out on the household staff. What had that maid done or said or forgotten to do? Whatever it was, the maid was treated as a good-for-nothing, a thief, or worse, and then Henriette fired her on the spot. The next day, she singled out another one, and the accusations ensued. An hour later, the maid was sent on her way without her final wages, as Henriette judged her unworthy of them. As one might imagine, neither maid was offered a letter of recommendation.

Henriette had been planning to reduce the household staff anyway, since it was costing her an arm and a leg. She had been thinking about it since the death of her husband and especially since her son started to bleed her dry with his two thousand francs a month. So, she did not replace the maids she fired. She also let the coachman go and sold the carriage and the horse. The only staff left in the house were Valentin Durieu, the butler, Céline Thébaud, the cook, Émilie Frasié, who took care of Louis de Marcillat, and four other maids, including Marie Pinaud and Stéphanie Parent. There was also a gardener who came twice a week. And they were costing her quite enough. She became more and more strict in dealing with them, more curt than ever.

She stopped attending high mass at the cathedral on Sundays and instead opted for the early morning mass at Saint-Porchaire, along with her staff. She still brought her daughter with her, accompanied by Marie Pinaud who was as strong as a man and could easily physically subdue Blanche if she ever thought to try to run off. Henriette had taught Marie not to trust Blanche and to always keep an eye on her. Marie Pinaud also considered the Lomet family to be the enemy. Because of this and her complete and total submission to Henriette Launier, she was paid more than the other maids.

Henriette Launier had been paying to reserve two pews: one at the cathedral and one at Saint-Porchaire. She wrote a letter to the bishop announcing that she no longer wished to reserve a pew at the cathedral and would no longer pay for it and that she would no longer help with the collection basket. From then on, she only attended Saint-Porchaire. It hurt her pride to write this letter, but it had to be done. The bishop, Paul Duillaume, who had known the family forever, was disappointed.

Ever since Honoré had yelled at her on the day he was demoted, Henriette Launier had cooled on the subject of her son. She also disliked her daughter-in-law, Maria-Teresa. The woman was of noble birth, that was true, but it was her only good quality. Henriette found her too coquettish, too lavish in her spending, too nonchalant, too much everything. Furthermore, her son's wife would raise her tone sometimes and did not hesitate to contradict her. And Maria-Teresa was especially annoying about asking to have Blanche spend a few days with them. Henriette had no desire to receive them in her house. With a wife like that, no wonder her son had become so irreverent and gotten so carried away. Because of his wife, he had become greedy. He was killing her with his two thousand francs a month, and now he wanted more!

Henriette Launier had understood quite clearly what her son had told her: if he ever lost his job, he would demand double the monthly allowance. As if he were entitled to that, the fool! But, she remembered, he was a lawyer after all, and she wasn't, and lawyers helped each other out. He might very well sue her and even hire Gilles Lomet as his attorney. Everyone said that the Lomets always won all of their cases. Could he be capable of that? Every time they talked about Républicains, Honoré would take their side. They couldn't get her daughter, so now they were coming for her son.

Honoré had threatened to demand more money if she held an elaborate Royalist funeral for his *grand-papa* like she did for his father. Henriette Launier would not make the same mistake twice, especially since that event was so expensive. No, for the funeral of Louis de Marcillat, she would do something simple, intimate, and everyone would understand her inner grief. Anyway, since her mother died, her father never went out or saw anyone anymore. Her son would not be coming to her to ask for more money.

Blanche's father was no longer there to take her on Sunday outings in the countryside. Her entire world was now limited to her room, the dining room, her grandfather's suite, and the back garden where she tended to her turtledoves.

She had lost her right to play piano some time ago. The door to the salon was always locked. It was only opened when Henriette Launier was present and just long enough for one of the maids to clean and dust. It wasn't even used to host guests anymore, since Henriette Launier no longer invited people over. When Letizia de Marcillat was alive, that room was never empty. When Martin Launier was alive, there was rarely a day when there wasn't at least one visitor.

Most of the guests had been Martin Launier's friends and acquaintances. His wife had usually been present when there were guests, listening politely and sometimes forming relationships with the wives who came along. But now that her husband was gone and her son was dishonored at work, she saw no reason to invite anyone to the house. Plus, hosting guests was costly. Looking back, she realized that the only reason she ever entertained was so that her husband could become a dean and her son could be promoted to prefect. Now her son was working in a prefecture where even the prefect was a Républicain. All hope was lost. There was no reason to invite anyone over except the inevitable Dr. Bauché who always showed up for lunch on Sundays. She needed to see him, for he was the only one who understood her.

There was actually another reason why Henriette Launier never invited people over anymore. The only people she knew were Royalists, and her son had made it quite clear that he could lose his job if she kept socializing with them: "If I lose my job, you'll have to double my allowance." He had spoken down to her that day, as if she were a servant. It irritated her, but she thought it was best to be prudent. So, she made sure not to invite anyone to the house who might harm her son's career and in doing so, ruin her financial situation.

She continued to receive invitations to visit others in her circle, and she'd just throw them in the fire, but not before taking the time to respond in writing that she couldn't possibly leave the house, that she and her daughter were both quite fatigued, and that her father was ill. In short, it was not possible to go out.

Louis de Marcillat spent his time in his quarters, sometimes in the company of his granddaughter. Since his fall, he found it painful and difficult to move around. Whenever Henriette saw him, all he did was complain—about Blanche's life, her future, and everything else—so, Henriette just avoided him. Émilie Frasié was always with him. He had everything he needed, and thankfully was not too demanding. As long as he had a supply of English tobacco and a bottle of alcohol, he was content.

Henriette never let it show, but she dreaded her father's rage. She was also scared that he might demand to see the lawyer and disinherit her so that Blanche could have the entire family fortune. She knew how much he loved his granddaughter. Deep down, she was simply afraid of the old man, so months would go by without her going upstairs to see him. Her father was eighty-three years old and had lived a long life. Maybe it was time for him to join his wife in heaven? He had adored Letizia and couldn't bear to even spend a day without her, so why was it taking so long for him to go join her? She shrugged, thinking that declarations of love were not so important after all.

The spring of 1883 was rotten. The winter hadn't been that cold, but now it was raining nonstop. It had been a year since Louis de Marcillat's son-in-law had died, though he never mourned the loss. Hearing from Émilie Frasié and Blanche about how gloomy the house was these days made him feel glum as well. Sitting in his armchair next to the window that looked over the garden, a drink on the table next to him, he watched the rain fall continuously, monotonously, pooling into large puddles below. He smoked his pipe pensively, waiting for Blanche to come read to him or talk to him about the good old days.

In the mornings, Émilie Frasié would help him to bathe and change clothes, which he disliked. He wanted to take care of himself, to take care of his own body, but ever since his fall on the stairs, he was incapable of that. His son-in-law was twenty years younger than him when he died. It was strange to think about that. Would he bury his daughter Henriette as well, or would she be the one to take him to the cemetery? What would become of Blanche after his death? His daughter and Blanche never got along well. They never understood each other, and his death would not make them develop a closer relationship. He could see that Henriette was a lot like him; she didn't like to go out, socializing exhausted her. She only got involved in political groups to please her husband when he was alive. Blanche was much more like Letizia. She loved to go out, to go to the seashore; long walks invigorated her, parties brought her to life, watching trials at the courthouse entertained her. She and her grandmother enjoyed the same things. Blanche had been happy when Letizia was alive.

With regret, Louis de Marcillat poured himself another glass of liquor. It was not his first drink of the day, nor would it be his last. Sometimes, he would finish off a whole bottle in one day. As he started to drink more and more, he was often quite intoxicated by six o'clock in the evening. On those days, he frightened Blanche. Even though he would never turn on her, he looked nothing like the *grand-papa* she knew and loved. Completely sloshed, his hair sticking up in all directions, a scowl on his face, his shirt disheveled with the sleeves pulled up, he looked like one of those drunks she used to see stumbling out of a tavern. Watching her grandfather destroy himself like this often made her cry. She would hide in her room, unable to help him in those moments. The problem was that Louis de Marcillat was an angry drunk. You could hear him yelling from every room in the house. Usually, he'd take aim at his daughter, threatening to disinherit her for good. After he let it all out, he would collapse onto his bed and pass out. As soon as Émilie Frasié heard him begin to snore, she'd place a blanket over him so he wouldn't get cold.

One morning, Henriette Launier went upstairs to see him. Again, Louis de Marcillat brought up Blanche's suffering:

"The girl is suffocating in this house. She's always alone. She needs to see people. Let her go spend some time with her brother."

"We will go visit him together."

"Blanche is not a child. She's thirty-four years old. Don't keep her on a leash like a dog!"

"Mind your own business!"

"You are a tyrant, a horrible mother. You're suffocating her, and you'll end up killing her. Yes, you'll kill her."

"Shut up, old man. You're not in your right mind and have no idea what's going on."

"It's your fault that she has asthma."

"Nonsense. She has a garden, a beautiful room, all the books she could ever want to read, her embroidery, a whole house to wander around."

"When you were her age, did your mother and I treat you like this?"

"Times have changed. The world is more dangerous today. Out in the world, there is violence. And, anyway, when I was her age, I was married with two children."

"Whose fault is it that Blanche is not married? You refused her suitor."

"Oh, don't start with that Lomet fellow. You know very well that Républicain rat is the reason why Honoré lost his post at the prefecture."

Louis de Marcillat found these arguments very tiring. There was nothing he could do to help his little Blanche and if he were to push it, he might even lose her. He was pained after each encounter with his daughter. He knew she was capable of stopping Blanche from coming to see him, and he needed Blanche like he needed air to breathe. He wished he were ten years younger, with Letizia by his side. His daughter wouldn't have dared to talk back to him then. Now he was old and virtually powerless. She was in control. Unable to help the one person he loved more than any other, his beautiful granddaughter, the poor old man drowned himself in liquor.

After yet another argument with his daughter, Louis de Marcillat suddenly fell ill. Since this was a rare occurrence, Blanche got scared and stayed by his side all day. The turtledoves would have to figure out some other way to get food and water from that day on.

Blanche's *grand-papa* was not well at all. Dr. Bauché came to see him and wanted to hospitalize him at the Hôtel-Dieu, but the old man got so angry about the idea that his daughter did not insist. Anyway, she thought, it might be better for him to die at home rather than in a hospital. It was a rare occasion when both father and daughter agreed.

He was in agony for days on end. Day and night, he had a hard time breathing. The doctor prescribed morphine, which offered some relief, but once it wore off, the stabbing pain in his chest would return worse than before.

During rare moments of calm, he would have liked to smoke his pipe, but his daughter adamantly opposed the idea. To dissuade him, she told him it was better he didn't light up his pipe because he might cause a fire in the house.

Blanche surmised that her mother was just trying to thwart her grandfather's wishes, so she secretly prepared the pipe for him, throwing out the old tobacco and adding and packing down a fresh pinch. She would light it for him and hand it to him to take small puffs. But sometimes it would cause the old man to have a coughing fit. The coughing was so loud that Henriette would come charging up the stairs. Blanche would have to fly to the window and swing it wide open to let out the tobacco smell, hide the pipe, and wait for her mother to leave the room. Grandfather and granddaughter remained accomplices, and when Henriette Launier appeared, they would act natural, pretending to be absorbed in a book. Henriette often wondered if she were just imagining things.

Grand-papa also often wanted a drink. Again, Blanche would be the one to serve it to him. She knew that Émilie Frasié would not approve and that the maid might also have to change the sheets because her grandfather frequently had accidents in bed, but she thought he needed alcohol to get better. She never once imagined that he might be about to pass away.

He had waves of intense pain that started to happen more and more frequently. Louis de Marcillat would be overcome with a guttural kind of wheezing and would cough up yellowish phlegm that he would spit into a pot held by Blanche. She would sit him up, holding him by the shoulders, until the coughing fit was over. It was not hard for her to hold him up now. When he was younger, he was a rather large man, but now he was just skin and bones. He had become very fragile; his body was telling him he was near the end.

Émilie Frasié knew what was happening and did really care for Louis de Marcillat. She would tell Blanche to take a break and go walk in the garden, to let him rest because there was nothing that she could do for him, especially when he was sleeping. But Blanche could not bring herself to leave him. She sat silently, watching her grandfather and waiting for him to wake up. She leafed through a photo album so that she would have some photos ready to show him the minute he opened his eyes. He loved that.

At one point, Émilie Frasié noticed that Blanche was crying and tried to comfort her, saying: "This is normal. It's how life is. He's going to join your grandmother." This just made her bawl even harder. She loved her grandfather as much as she had loved her grandmother. They had grown closer after her grandmother's death. And now he was going to leave her too! She couldn't bring herself to think about him dying; she held out hope until he took his last breath. Each time Dr. Bauché came to see the old man, she'd ask him: "You can save him, right, Doctor? Don't you think he looks a little better today?"

But the end was near. Blanche dabbed her grandfather's lips with a wet cloth once an hour. She would feed him little spoonfuls of sugar water, as that was all he could consume. Each time he swallowed, he'd moan in pain.

One morning, Henriette Launier called for Father Mallouet to come administer the last rites to her father. That day, Louis de Marcillat was feeling a little better, and with an enigmatic smile, he welcomed the priest dressed in his surplice. He felt the irony of this moment given that he hadn't even laid eyes on a priest in years.

Father Mallouet spritzed him with holy water, and he did not flinch. He lowered the crucifix asking Louis de Marcillat to kiss it and to appeal to the mercy of Christ. The old man spoke softly. Father Mallouet blessed him and prayed for him. Together they recited the Our Father prayer, along with Blanche, who had tears running down her cheeks. Then Blanche left the room so that the priest could hear her grandfather's final confession. Louis de Marcillat requested that a mass be said for him, which the priest agreed to do.

Blanche was not happy with her mother's decision to do this. She pulled her aside and said: "What made you call for Father Mallouet? This type of visit is going to kill him! The last rites should only be administered to people who are dying. Grandfather is not dying."

Henriette Launier did not respond. She just shrugged her shoulders. It was the first time her daughter had come downstairs in ten days. She figured that it would soon be over, and that Blanche, as usual, had no comprehension of what was happening. That girl really would never understand anything.

Louis de Marcillat's breathing became labored. Blanche studied his face, trying to engrave it in her memory. Drops of rain were hitting the window panes and a strong wind was blowing down through the chimney, making an eerie noise. Once in a while, the old man would crack his eyes open, looking for something or someone. When he saw his granddaughter, who was holding his hand, he would squeeze her hand gently. With long sighs, he looked into her eyes and saw the sad reality of what was happening. Sometimes Blanche would hug him with all of her might, her face bathed in warm tears.

In the garden, raindrops continued to fall on the trees, and little flower petals from the apple tree fluttered off in the wind. Blanche had not slept for two nights. Oddly, she looked a lot like her grandmother had looked when she was in her final hours. She gazed into the eyes of her beloved *grand-papa*. Thin sideburns outlined his pale face. In just a few days, he had lost all of his hair. Blanche wiped the sweat from his bald head with dry towels. By tending to him so affectionately, she was trying to hold on to something real, something durable and eternal.

Suddenly, he sat up, leaning slightly forward. His contorted face frozen, his cheeks hollower than before, he extended his arms saying, "Letizia!" Blanche was trembling, with beads of sweat running down her face. She didn't think to blow her nose, and mucus dribbled from her nostrils as she propped up the pillows behind her grandfather.

She heard the church bells toll three times. The sun would be coming up soon. Leaning against the pillows, Louis de Marcillat's arms fell down off the sides of the bed. His mouth agape, he sucked in big breaths of air. With difficulty, he spoke again: "Blanche!" But he could not see her. He called for her but could not see her bright eyes staring into his. His neck muscles tensed and his head fell back.

All that could be heard was the crackling of the fire, the rain hitting the window, and the splitter-splatter of large drops falling into the turtledove cage down in the garden. It was an interminable April night.

Finally, he fell asleep again, eyes half open.

Blanche added a log to the fire. She had already fed the fire at least half a dozen times that night. Piled together, the burning logs gave off a soft, warm heat. The fire crackled continuously, interrupted only by an occasional gust of wind that would blow down the chimney and momentarily subdue the flames. Seeing her grandfather so frail, Blanche could no longer hold back and began to sob. She pulled the covers up over him, making sure not to wake him. Completely drained, she curled up under a blanket in the armchair and listened to the rain fall without ever taking her eyes off of her grandfather.

Without him, life had no meaning. She stretched out her arms to warm her hands by the fire. It was burning brightly and casting reassuring shadows in the room. She added another log, brushing aside the burnt embers. Sparks sprayed into the room, floating up, crisscrossing, and slowly drifting down towards her. The laurel branches, chosen purposely by her grandfather's maid, filled the room with a pleasant scent meant to ward off death.

Louis de Marcillat's face darkened in the shadows.

Suddenly, he lifted his head like a raptor, his nostrils flaring, the stark angles of his face contorted in the large shadows on the wall. Concerned, Blanche stood up, her heart beating fiercely. Her grandfather's shoulders began to shake in a worrisome way. His unnaturally raised eyebrows seemed to be seeking an answer to a question, while his hunched shoulders straightened up. His bulging chest let out a loud cry, and the old man fell back onto the bed.

Blanche heard an odd sound she had never heard before. Beside herself, she flung her full weight against her grandfather's body, convulsing as she clutched him as tightly as she could.

In the morning, Émilie Frasié found them like this. She wanted to close the dead man's eyelids but couldn't get to them. She peeled Blanche's arms off of the body. Blanche released her grip and fainted.

The burial was a horrible ordeal for Blanche, who came down the stairs behind the morticians sobbing and wailing. Dr. Bauché was there and had a vial of laudanum in his pocket. He administered some to Blanche and then gave the vial to Henriette Launier so she could dole it out to her whenever she felt it was necessary.

Louis de Marcillat's funeral was not held in the cathedral, but in Saint-Porchaire Church. Old Father Mallouet led the funeral mass. It had been more than ten years since Louis de Marcillat had been to his church, and no one had seen him in any other church either. His wife Letizia had died eleven years ago, and for the past ten years he hadn't left his suite in the family mansion except to go to the hospital the one time he broke his leg.

Father Mallouet had made his peace with him after he confessed his sins and reconciled with God not long ago. He was not a resentful man, so he gave a beautiful homily at the mass. Although Louis de Marcillat had not been attending weekly mass for years, it should be noted that his daughter Henriette had made up for her father's lapses by spending her Sundays at Saint-Porchaire attending mass and vespers, saying the rosary, and participating in evening prayers.

During the funeral mass, Henriette Launier had to elbow her daughter several times to get her to participate, to give the right responses to the priest's prayers, and to sing along with everyone, but Blanche wasn't up to it. She either didn't speak or she spoke at the wrong time. Even worse, when the priest said, "Louis, you have gone to join your wife Letizia," Blanche fainted.

Ashamed, her mother acted as if she didn't notice. Émilie Frasié had to revive her.

Henriette Launier was miffed at her daughter for making such a spectacle of herself in front of strangers. There were people at the mass that Henriette didn't know or only recognized by sight. They obviously knew her father and had read the obituary in the newspapers that indicated when the funeral would be held. They must be people of good standing in society, and she feared Blanche's antics might cause people to gossip about them. If Blanche were to attract that kind of attention, she would never forgive her. Once again, she looked at her clueless daughter with condescension.

During the mass, she tried to concentrate on her prayers, determined to give her father a decent burial. She did love him, and even if they often disagreed, they understood one another. Their only real bone of contention was about how to manage Blanche.

After mass, given the small number of attendees, Henriette Launier asked everyone to get into their coaches and meet at the cemetery. For the sake of her son, and so that she wouldn't have to double his allowance, she had agreed to a small ceremony restricted to close family and friends. She had no desire to march up the cobblestone street on foot, too ashamed to make a spectacle of this pathetic funeral.

The ceremony at the cemetery was without pageantry. The family stood around the grave, behind them were the known and unknown guests, and further back stood the entire household staff. Father Mallouet concluded his remarks stating: "Louis, you were born of dust and to dust you shall return." When they lowered the casket into the grave, Blanche fainted again. And once again, Henriette Launier pretended not to notice. How dare that girl ruin the last moments of her father's journey! Émilie Frasié pulled Blanche back behind the crowd and laid her next to a cypress tree while patting her cheeks and trying to revive her. She missed the end of the ceremony.

Father Mallouet sang the prayer for the deceased and psalm 129 to ensure that his parishioner would ascend into heaven. Henriette Launier, her nose in the missal, followed along and sang: "From the depths of the abyss, I called for you, Lord. Lord, hear my voice... May you hear my prayer... Lord, grant him eternal rest, may your light shine upon him... May he rest in peace. Amen."

Blanche was greatly affected by the loss of her grandfather, but his death had the odd result of bringing her closer to her mother. It was just the two of them in the house now. Although she rarely left her room, she would go downstairs to the dining room at mealtime, at least for lunch, since she was rarely hungry in the evening.

Henriette was yet again, and this time critically, faced with the thorny issue of inheritance. She knew that her father had filed a last will and testament with his lawyer some time ago, but she did not know what it said, and she was concerned. She knew that her mother had left everything she owned to Blanche. Until his death, her father had legal control of the funds, but now it was time to settle accounts.

She decided to delay the reading of the will while she attempted to win over her daughter. She knew that Blanche loved oysters, so she ordered some from the best fishmonger in the city.

She would go up to Blanche's room quite frequently and was all sweetness and light when they spoke. One afternoon, she finally broached the topic.

"You know that you and your brother are my only heirs."

"Let's not speak of this, *maman*."

"On the contrary, we must. Do you need anything? Are you comfortable here?"

"Of course, I have everything I need, and you are spoiling me with these oysters. They're so delicious."

"You know that your grandmother left everything to you. But I know that you truly loved your *grand-maman* and that you wouldn't dare sully her memory by squabbling about money, right?"

"That's correct. I don't need anything."

"I think it's best if I take care of all of that. Do you trust me?"

"Yes, of course."

"Fine, then we will go to see the lawyer soon. I will invest your grandmother's money, and when I die, the fortune will have grown so much that you will never want for anything."

She provided a lengthy explanation of why it was in Blanche's best interest to sign a paper giving her control of the money. Blanche listened, but really had no interest in money. What would she do with it? How could this inheritance benefit her? She still missed her grandmother and was happy to be rid of an inheritance that she didn't know what to do with. Her mother had struck the right note, and it had worked perfectly. Blanche did not want her memories of her grandparents to be overshadowed by discussions about money. All she could think about was her grief. All she wanted were her grandmother's things and some mementos of her grandfather. She had taken out Letizia de Marcillat's black dresses and only went down to the dining room fully dressed in mourning, wearing a black pearl necklace as her grandmother used to do in times like these. Once she had all of her grandmother's clothes and the camera and photographs that belonged to her grandfather, there was nothing more she needed.

Henriette Launier brought her daughter, dressed in mourning, to the lawyer's office. Maître Billedoux had recently passed away as well, so they met with a younger lawyer, Maître Pelletier. Henriette Launier found the reading of the will to be arduous. Her father had left everything to her, but included a clause requiring her to purchase a two-story house for Honoré. She would continue to own the property and her son would live in it. Upon her death, Honoré would inherit the house. This was another blow for Henriette. She would have liked to skip over that section, but the lawyer refused, as did Honoré: "Fine, mother, I will not ask you to increase my allowance, but rent is expensive. I want the house."

As soon as Henriette Launier received the inheritance money, she purchased a two-story house on Rue de la Visitation, directly across from her own mansion. It was a solid, spacious, traditional home, typical of the historic buildings one might find in Poitiers today. Honoré Launier no longer had to pay rent, and he did not ask for an increase to his allowance.

Although she was not happy that she had to purchase this home for her son, Henriette Launier started to feel better about her situation. She had received her inheritance and felt relieved at first and later fully satisfied. Blanche had signed the document prepared by Maître Pelletier. Henriette was now fully in control. Sure, she had been in control of the money ever since her mother died because her father always gave her free rein and let her manage the household as she saw fit. But now, no one could question her. Her only responsibility was to her own conscience, and her conscience was never bothered.

She had skillfully taken everything away from her daughter, but even she didn't realize it because, in her mind, she had only acted in the girl's best interest. And when she had asked her daughter if she needed or wanted anything, the girl had plainly stated that she needed nothing. She had everything she wanted.

Honoré Launier was also quite content. Ten years ago, his grandmother had left everything to Blanche, and he thought that was unfair since doing so meant that he had been disinherited. His grandfather had rebalanced the scale. Honoré was not unaware of his mother's manipulations, but his sister was thirty-five years old and never went out. It seemed unlikely she would ever marry. So, what more could she want?

Henriette Launier had stripped her daughter of her inheritance, but she wasn't a total monster. She allowed Blanche to have all of her parents' personal belongings and spoiled her when it came to meals. And for a woman who detested frivolous spending, that took some real effort. Blanche would enjoy hot chocolate in the morning, oysters or filet of sole or cutlets at noon, and in the evening, she would often have brioche. These were all of her favorites.

Henriette Launier had every reason to be happy with this outcome. The house that her son and daughter-in-law occupied across the street had cost her a pretty penny, but it had appeased her greedy son, and she swore to herself that it was the last time she would be taken like that.

Finally, she resolved to bring some order to her household. A butler, a cook, four maids, a maid for her father who was now gone... all this was too much for two women living alone. She decided to make some cuts to the staff. She called everyone together and gave a little speech about how expensive things were and how she now had a reduced budget because her father was gone, a speech that no one believed because they knew full well how strong the family's financial situation was, and then she announced she was firing the butler, Valentin

Durieu, and two maids that she insisted she could no longer afford. She gave them each their final wages and strong letters of recommendation she had prepared in advance.

～

October 1884

Firing half of the staff did not make Henriette Launier any less demanding of those who remained. She felt the need to give the house a deep cleaning. She became obsessive about cleanliness and tidiness, making sure the only smell in the house was that of furniture polish. Her maids never had a minute of free time. Stéphanie Parent, the oldest one, was not accustomed to this much activity. At one point, worn out, she went downstairs to have a piece of bread with jam. Henriette Launier caught her in the kitchen. Enraged, she abruptly announced that the maid was fired and was to leave the house that evening.

Ever since Louis de Marcillat's death, Stéphanie Parent had grown tired of Henriette Launier. The woman kept tabs on everything the maids ate, and often didn't give them enough time to finish their meals. She would not miss working in this house. The only down-side was leaving without a letter of recommendation. But Henriette Launier would not get off scot-free. After all, it was Stéphanie Parent who had accompanied Henriette, Blanche, and Marie Pinaud to the Protestant church for the fake marriage of Gilles Lomet… and Stéphanie Parent would make good use of this information.

Quietly, the maid went up to Blanche's room, entered, and told her point-blank: "I have something to tell you. I can't lie to you anymore. Your mother made up the story about Maître Lomet. He's not married."

Blanche leapt up from her seat: "You're lying! I saw the wedding!"

"That was someone else's wedding. It was your mother's idea."

Blanche, devastated, fell back in her chair muttering, "It can't be true!"

Stéphanie Parent insisted: "It is true. He's as unmarried as one can be. I know because my cousin had an issue with his landlord always raising the rent, so he went to consult with Maître Lomet just last week. I know for sure that he is not married."

"But, that's insane!"

"I swear I am telling the truth. He is still single. It was your mother's idea, I assure you."

Once Stéphanie Parent had left the room, Blanche sat still for a moment on the edge of her bed. The more time passed, the more she was filled with an overwhelming sense of joy. She was bursting with happiness: Gilles was single, he hadn't betrayed her, her life wasn't over! She looked at herself in the mirror and saw a dreary woman in black. She ran to her grandmother's room and flung open the armoire. She took out one of her grandmother's prettiest dresses, a bright-colored party dress, for today was a day to celebrate. She brought the dress back to her room and feverishly filled a travel bag with necessities: hairbrush, nightgown, an everyday dress, a shawl... She had made up her mind. She was going to leave tomorrow! She would wait until her mother was out of the house running errands, and then she'd slip out. She would go to Gilles, and they would get married, whether her mother liked it or not!

Although it was not her usual routine, she went down to the dining room that evening and was cheerful and kind to her mother. She even gave her a kiss before heading back up to bed, which she hadn't done since the day her mother had forbidden her to play the piano. Henriette Launier went to bed happy that night, thinking her daughter was finally in a good mood for once.

Blanche was over the moon. She couldn't wait to leave. She planned to go find Gilles, and she was sure he would welcome her with open arms. After all these years of silence between them, he never married. He must be waiting for her. She was as sure about that as she was about her own feelings. She spent the entire night dreaming about their future. She forgot about losing her grandmother and then her grandfather. She was no longer in mourning; she was engaged! She was still a young girl at heart, and she was the one Gilles Lomet was waiting for.

All night long, she wondered what he had been doing during the ten years they were apart. In her mind, he hadn't changed a bit and was still handsome, attentive, loving... She also remembered his mother, whom she had visited for tea on Sunday afternoons and who was also very warmhearted; she had welcomed her into their home as if she were already a daughter-in-law. She could picture the salon where they had tea, the knick-knacks on the table, the piano she would play at Madame Lomet's request. It had been ten years since she had played the piano! She wondered if she still knew how. What had she done for the past ten years? What would she have to talk about? Her memories of the wonderful evenings she spent with her grandfather were fading. How would she describe these ten years of her life?

It had been ten years since she watched Gilles argue a case in court. He was probably still just as good, better even, now that he had more experience. How many cases had he brought to trial since the last time she went to the Palais de Justice? They had ten years of experiences to catch up on. She felt young again. Her grandmother had always told her she was built for childbearing: with her wide hips, the babies would slide right out. Gilles had always talked about wanting children.

She got up several times that night and lit a candle to look at herself in the mirror and reassure herself that she was still pretty. She put on her most beautiful dress and looked at herself from every angle in the candlelight. Finally, she went back to bed and slept like a log. The next morning, neither the daylight nor the street noise roused her. She didn't wake up until nine o'clock when

Émilie Frasié bellowed: *"Bonjour, mam'selle Blanche!"* It took her a few minutes to remember that today was going to be a big day.

Blanche ate her breakfast in a daze. In her mind, she was already gone, and she gave monosyllabic answers to all of her mother's questions. Then, she went back up to her room. When the clock struck ten, Henriette Launier and Marie Pinaud headed out on their errands with their baskets, as was their custom. They'd be gone for at least an hour, and that was more than enough time for her to escape. She waited fifteen minutes, just to be sure they were out of sight, then went downstairs with her travel bag, placing it in the vestibule before going to get Céline Thébaud to open the main door to the house. As usual, her mother had locked it with a key.

Céline Thébaud did indeed have a copy of the key, just in case someone came to the door, like the postman, or if there was a delivery, or an emergency like a fire, etc. Blanche was not an emergency. The maid was startled by the travel bag in the vestibule, but Blanche explained that she was going to her brother's house and that she wanted the door unlocked.

"He just lives across the street, *mam'selle* Blanche. You can wait for your mother to come home to go over there."

Blanche begged her, but nothing worked. She wouldn't open the door without the lady of the house being present. Like everyone else, Céline Thébaud knew about Blanche's love affair with Gilles Lomet, and she disapproved of it. At that moment, she wasn't thinking about him, though, for she thought that book had been closed. She thought Blanche's desire to visit her brother was just a passing whim and that it was best not to unlock the door for fear of incurring Madame's wrath and getting fired. She went back to her chores.

Blanche was upset, but not discouraged. She had made up her mind that she was going to leave, no matter what. So, she stood there waiting for her mother to return, ready for a confrontation. When Henriette Launier and Marie Pinaud returned with their baskets full, Blanche was there by the door, her travel bag at her feet.

"I'm leaving!" she said.

Her mother had just come through the door and Marie Pinaud, with her hefty stature, was blocking it.

"Where are you going?"

"To Honoré's house."

"With a travel bag?"

"I want to show some dresses to Maria-Teresa."

"Very well, we will go together in a few minutes."

"I don't need you to take me. I'm going now."

"I'll say it again: we will go together in a few minutes."

"Let me leave!"

"No! Only disreputable girls go out alone. You will wait for me."

"I want to leave! You hear me? I want to leave!"

"Leave? You've lost your mind."

Blanche was taller and bigger than her mother and could have pushed her out of the way to get through the door, but Céline Thébaud and the tank-like Marie Pinaud were holding her back, swearing at her. Blanche fought with them, yelling that she was free and that they had no right to stop her from leaving, that it was unfair, that they must let her go, but it was futile. She called the three of them every bad name she knew as they pushed her towards the stairs and forced her back up into her room. Marie Pinaud locked the door to her room, and it would remain so "until she comes to her senses."

This was the first time Blanche was locked in her room. Held captive, once and for all.

Blanche yelled and banged her fists on the door all day long. That day, she didn't eat or drink anything. That night, she didn't sleep, and the second day, after an asthma attack, she stopped yelling and asked for something to drink. Her mother sent her up a glass of water with some ether in it, one-fifth of the glass to be exact. She added some almond syrup to mask the taste. Blanche did continue to holler, but it began to sound more like begging and pleading. Between the shuttered window and the locked door, Blanche felt like she was suffocating. It was unbearable. She was panting like a dog, with quick short breaths and felt she might be dying… She started shouting again, not to demand that she be free to leave the house, but just to have the door to her room unlocked. As time progressed, she complained less about having her freedom taken away and more about how horrible her mother was.

The third day, exhausted, she didn't make a sound. She pressed her nose against the shutter, wrapped in a big shawl, imagining a thousand and one ways to escape. Since the banging and yelling had stopped, Henriette Launier sent up some food, which Blanche refused to eat. Her mother also sent up more water, again laced with ether and almond syrup. That afternoon, as expected, Blanche called for her mother and asked for her to come upstairs. From behind the door, she apologized to her mother and begged her let some air in the room. Henriette Launier made her daughter repeat several times that she was sorry for what she had done and that she would never do it again. Blanche obeyed. She forced herself to say the words her mother wanted to hear.

Strangely, Henriette Launier enjoyed listening to her say those words. She took advantage of the moment to ask why Blanche suddenly had this desire to leave home: "Why in heaven's name were you so intent on going to your brother's house without me?" Emotionally and physically exhausted, Blanche finally admitted that she wanted to leave so that she could be with Gilles Lomet and they could be married.

"You must be crazy!" her mother said, "Now you want to marry a married man?"

"You're lying. He's not married. He never was."

"You've lost your mind, and now you're losing your memory. You were with me when we saw the wedding take place."

"That wasn't his wedding. That was when Marie Girard and Marcellin Berthelot got married."

"Who told you such nonsense?"

"Stéphanie Parent did."

Henriette Launier swore up and down that the maid had lied to Blanche to get revenge for being fired.

"She didn't lie to me. She gave me her word."

"What good is the word of a maid? She'd swear on a Bible for any little trifle. And you'd rather believe a maid than your own mother?"

Blanche stopped insisting since the argument was getting her nowhere. She no longer believed anything her mother said. She could hear in her mother's voice that she was lying. As instructed, she promised not to carry on anymore, to stop yelling and begging for help. "You know that when people yell like that, the police come to arrest them and take them away to prison. Did you know that?" Blanche listened and began to feel afraid. If her mother could lie to her like that, what else was she capable of? She resolved to stop yelling and to start coming up with a plan. She would have to find a way to escape so she could be with Gilles.

Blanche started eating less and less. In no time, she had lost five kilos. She was too sad to be hungry. Her mother continued to assert that Gilles really was married, and to keep the peace, she pretended to believe her. In reality, she was hoping her mother would forget what she had tried to do so that she would loosen her grip a little and Blanche might find a way to escape.

In the afternoon, Blanche would say she was tired and needed a nap. It was just a pretext to be able to have time alone in her room so that she could write to Gilles Lomet. In her letters, she explained how they were stopping her from leaving, how they took away her freedom, how they shuttered her window and kept her in the dark. She told all the details of her sad and desperate state. She would then put the letters into envelopes and shoot them through the slats of the shutter like messages in a bottle tossed into the sea. They would float down onto the sidewalk or be swept into the street. She knew they wouldn't be delivered, but hoped against hope that one day someone might pick up one of the letters and bring it to Gilles. She just had to keep trying.

When Henriette Launier realized that her daughter was slipping letters out of her window again, she decided to put an end to it once and for all by contriving a scheme to scare her. She pulled aside the gardener, Constant Pichu, and explained what she wanted him to do. She had him bang loudly on the door, yelling "Police, open up!" while she ran up to Blanche's room to tell her that the police were there to take her away for bad behavior. She reminded Blanche that her father had been a respected dean of the Faculté des Lettres and that she herself was known to all as a good mother, an honest woman, and a faithful parishioner. Anyone could confirm it.

While the fake policeman bellowed below, Henriette Launier continued: "Did anyone force you to sign that power of attorney document?" Blanche admitted they had not. Now suffering from chronic malnourishment, the young girl truly believed her mother had called the police to take her away.

"Do you want to go to prison, daughter, or should I tell them that you will stop accusing your parents of such ridiculous things? You know you can't attack your parents without some kind of punishment."

Blanche promised to stop writing letters and to obey her mother. Later, thinking back on this moment, Blanche realized that her mother was indeed a well-known person in society and that everyone would believe her mother if she told them that it was for Blanche's own good that she never left home. No one would believe her story. Blanche swore to herself that she would never go after her mother in court. What she wanted, all she wanted, was to be with Gilles. She had no interest in any of the rest.

Blanche started going downstairs for meals again, and things started to get back to normal. One afternoon, she was wandering around her grandparents' suite. Her grandfather's room looked out onto the back garden, which was enclosed. There was no way to escape from there. But her grandmother's old room and the library both had windows facing the street. That day, she had no interest in reading a book or trying on one of her grandmother's dresses. She might not be able to escape from her own room, but from here, it was indeed possible.

The rooms on the ground floor were always locked at night, but her grandparents' suite on the third floor wasn't. The only problem was that it was so high up! She had to find a way to get to the street from the third floor. There were no gutters on the front of the house; they were all on the garden side. What she needed was a rope.

Blanche had read several novels where the hero broke out of prison by climbing down a rope. She just had to find one. Constant Pichu kept one in the garden shed. Taking every possible precaution, and with luck on her side, she was able to evade her mother's vigilant eye and get her hands on the gardener's coil of thick rope. She hurried it up to her room and hid it under her bed. She then spent several days putting knots in the rope at regular intervals, something she had read about in a book. When the rope was ready, Blanche moved to the next stage in her plan.

For the next few nights, she would observe the household and make note of people's routines: what time everyone went to bed, especially her mother, and at what time it became totally silent. Her mother's room was just below hers, so she would have to be careful. The maids' chambers were on the top floor, just above her. When the whole house fell silent, she used a candle to check the time on her grandfather's old pocket watch.

After two nights, she couldn't hold back any longer. She put on a sweater and cotton pants meant to go under a dress, but without the bulky skirts that might get in her way. Rope in hand, she tiptoed over to her grandmother's room, making sure not to let any floorboards squeak. She tied one end of the rope to a heavy piece of furniture and threw the other end out the window. Then, she climbed out and started to make her way down.

She lowered herself one knot at a time, and all was going well. She was escaping! About half way down to the ground, she stretched her feet down but could not find another knot. She had run out of rope. The sidewalk was illuminated by a streetlight; it was too far down to jump. She would have to go back up and find a way to lengthen the rope. The escape would have to be put on hold. Climbing back up sounded easy, but it was not. She just couldn't do it. She had sufficient strength to lower herself down, but enough not to pull herself up. She tried in vain until fatigue and vertigo set in and she started to shake. She began to cry and moan, quietly at first, and then to stammer: "Help. Help me, please." Émilie Frasié, who slept with her window open, heard her.

In less than five minutes, the whole house was awake. Together, Marie Pinaud, Émilie Frasié, Céline Thébaud, and Henriette Launier were able to pull Blanche back up to the window. Blanche collapsed onto the floor, as her mother called for a whip. Helped by the two maids who held Blanche in place, Henriette gave her a lashing right then and there. Blanche was whipped twenty times that night and was bleeding when she was led back to her room. That very night, they moved Émilie Frasié's bed into Blanche's room, and Blanche would never be alone at night again. Henriette Launier also locked up her parents' suite and had someone block up all of the cracks in Blanche's shuttered window.

VII

1883–1885: The Lomet family

Maître Jacob Lomet consistently voted to approve all of Jules Ferry's laws. Given the number of new laws proposed, this certainly kept him busy. He was most happy during his second term as Council President when, from 1883 to 1885, Jules Ferry enacted his plan to consolidate and strengthen a government made up of Républicains. Maître Lomet never tired of singing Jules Ferry's praises and never stopped penning articles in support of him. Like Ferry, who was also a lawyer, he worried about the power held by judges who, for the most part, were Royalists. So, when Jules Ferry went on the offensive against judges and eliminated lifetime appointments, Maître Lomet was ecstatic.

In the elder Lomet's eyes, Jules Ferry was the right man for the moment. He was particularly enthusiastic about France's colonial expansion which, under Ferry, was at its height. France was exporting its military might around the globe, preceded by explorers and scientists whose mission was to find uncivilized societies to enlighten. They spread through Madagascar, West Africa, Tunisia, the Sahara, Vietnam.

Wherever they went, they were met with fierce resistance by the local populations, but none of that news made it back to the general public in France. In Vietnam, for example, offensives launched by the Black Flag Army resulted in huge losses for the French troops during the conquest of Tonkin, including killing some of their best men like Francis Garnier and naval officer Henri Rivière. Those facts, however, never made it out of the hushed offices of the French government ministers. What was printed in the newspapers was that France kept winning, conquering one territory after another, inspiring Jacob Lomet to pick up his pen. He wrote an article praising the French army when he learned that Tunisia had signed a treaty making it a protectorate of France. No one knew of the bloody battles fought against Ahmadou and Samory to topple ancient kingdoms in West Africa. No one knew of the years of combat necessary to defeat the Tuareg resistance in North Africa. Jacob Lomet didn't know any better than any of his compatriots in France. He believed the likes of Savorgnan de Brazza who, in between colonial expeditions, would travel around France boasting about the army's accomplishments. Like him, Jacob Lomet believed that France's colonial expansion was beneficial to the "natives" who would now have access to civilization, modernity, and democracy.

Savorgnan de Brazza would never mention the forced labor demanded of these new French citizens in order to complete elaborate construction projects. Neither did Jacob Lomet, who wrote with conviction: "We bring these poor souls our methods, our medicines, our democratic ideals." Articles about far-off countries were all the rage, as the French craved all that was "exotic." Readers devoured them, and Républicains saw them as a way to win over voters. The aspirations of the Second Empire were nothing compared to those of this Third Republic.

For Jacob Lomet and others like him, Jules Ferry was a hero. So, when he was almost assassinated by a radical at the Palais Bourbon, there was a public outcry. Jacob Lomet called an assembly of local Républicains that very evening. Standing on the platform with tears in his eyes, he fired up the large crowd that had gathered, saying: "When anarchy strikes at the heart of our democracy, threatening us all by attacking one of our best men, it hurts every one of us. We agonize with him, his wife, and his children. Why, I ask you, is there so much hate in this country?"

As for the Royalists, they were not agonizing one bit. Jules Ferry had become so unpopular among them due to his anticlerical laws that when he finally left office, they all popped open their best bottles of champagne.

Though Gilles Lomet was a Républicain, he did not agree with all of his father's political beliefs. Far from it. He had attended a Catholic school as a child because there were no Protestant schools in Poitiers then and had made good friends in the Catholic community. When he went to law school, he further widened his circle of friends. Also, in his career as a lawyer, he worked with people of both faiths, never discriminating when it came to clients. But really, it was his love for Blanche that had made him a more tolerant man. For her, he was even willing to put his own faith second so that their children could be raised Catholic.

He agreed with Jules Ferry that there should be a school for boys and a school for girls in every town, and that education should be free and non-religious, but he would have preferred that this occur peacefully, without completely disbanding all of the Catholic schools. He believed that people should be able to choose and that public schooling should be free and accessible for those without means. He was more interested in social issues than political ones, and the older he got, the more he leaned in that direction. Further, he was not at all convinced that all this warmongering to conquer new lands was necessary. It reminded him of the Napoleonic campaigns and their sad outcomes. Like some French radical thinkers, he considered the military costs too high at a time when French people were suffering from poverty and unemployment. All that money could be used to help them. The articles that he wrote, for he wrote as well, were completely different from those of his father. When Louis Pasteur was being attacked, for example, he went all out to defend him.

What was the trouble with Pasteur? On July 6, 1885, little Joseph Meisteur was bitten by a dog who had rabies. Everyone thought he would die a painful death. Pasteur had been working on rabies for quite some time and had developed a vaccine that he had tested on healthy dogs, so he decided to use it to save the child. After a long month filled with doubts, the child finally recovered and was cured. In November, Pasteur tried to use the vaccine again, this time on a girl who had been bitten by a rabid dog, but the vaccine had been administered too late and the girl died. The conservative press, disapproving of Pasteur's methods, lashed out against him. Gilles Lomet defended him.

Pasteur was not deterred by these events. Sure of his work, he went to Russia, where he saved children who had been bitten by wolves. When he returned to Paris, Gilles Lomet went to meet with him and offered to support him. Together, they fought, one article after another. When Gilles was a boy, he had lost his best friend to rabies and that loss had stayed with him. One of the main articles he penned was aptly entitled *"Sauvons nos enfants!"*: save our children. In it, he argued so convincingly in favor of the vaccine that the cabal against Louis Pasteur fell silent.

～

November 1884

Because Blanche no longer had paper on which to express her desperation, she began writing on the walls of her room. Her suffering came out as:

Sortez-moi Seigneur de cet enfer! Lord, save me from this hell!

Vierge Marie, je suis votre servante, intercédez pour moi! Holy Mary, I am your servant, intercede on my behalf!

Vivre libre, pouvoir me promener près du Clain... To live free, to be able to walk by the Clain River...

Revoir la mer, une dernière fois... To see the ocean, one last time...

Sometimes, she would pray as well, though no one could hear her. She no longer went to Sunday mass, which used to be the only time she left the house. It had been her mother's decision: "You will be allowed back in church once you have come to your senses."

So, Blanche never left her room anymore. Whenever she felt the need, she would relieve herself in the chamber pot that was usually only used at night. Since it was rarely emptied, the room began to smell... Émilie Frasié brought her food three times a day, but she often skipped a meal, or three. Leftovers would fall on the bed or on the floor, as the young woman began to unravel. Overcome with distress, she let herself go. She wouldn't wash or change clothes, and she began to smell horribly bad, but she didn't even notice.

Sometimes, feeling better for a moment, she would be gripped with despair and wail violently, screaming that she was being buried alive. Henriette Launier was afraid that the neighbors or a visitor might hear her, even though there were no more visitors. Dr. Bauché was the only guest, still coming for a meal at the house once a week. It was strange that this doctor, who knew of Blanche's bad asthma, never once asked to see her or to go up to her room to examine her. Since she never came downstairs to eat and stayed in her room, and since her mother had explained that she spent all day lying on her bed in her nightgown, he deduced that the girl must be neurasthenic.

In reality, Henriette Launier had removed all of the dresses from Blanche's room so that if she ever thought to try to escape again or to ask anyone for help, she would be wearing her nightgown and everyone would think she was crazy. And that's exactly what happened. One day, Blanche wanted to speak with Dr. Bauché. She would have put on a dress but couldn't find one, so she went downstairs anyway. When she saw the doctor, she burst into tears. Dr. Bauché realized that Henriette Launier was right: her daughter was mentally ill. After that moment, Henriette felt she had nothing to fear. Whatever her daughter might say or do, Dr. Bauché would confirm that the girl had lost her faculties and needed to stay in the care of her mother.

Despite all of that drama, life went on, and Blanche started to feel a little better. One day, she asked for her clothes, and her mother gave her one dress. She washed, combed her hair, changed clothes, made herself look respectable, and went to talk to her mother.

"Let's go out, *maman*, I need to breathe fresh air. Let's go to Saint-Porchaire!"

"If you apologize and behave yourself from now until Sunday, we'll go then."

"I apologize. Forgive me for being a bad daughter."

Henriette Launier just loved these moments, when her daughter begged forgiveness, but the brief periods of submission never lasted. Eventually, she would start to scream and yell again, hoping that someone outside might hear her and come to her aide. The neighbors actually had heard her, but they all believed the stories circulated by the maids, that the girl was overwrought and had lost her senses.

Blanche's anger eventually reached a fever pitch. At one point, she grabbed her mother's wrists and with flashes of rage in her dark eyes she yelled: "Are you going to let me leave, yes or no? Wretched woman!" This really scared Henriette Launier. She called for help, and Marie Pinaud came running. The maid pulled Blanche away from her mother, and Blanche finally let go of her mother's wrists. As her mother and the maid descended the staircase, Blanche snatched up her chamber pot and threw it down at them.

Henriette Launier could no longer tolerate her daughter's rebelliousness, so she often kept the girl's room locked from the outside. Blanche's despair was overwhelming. She threw herself at the door to try to escape, hitting it so hard that she broke it. Henriette Launier called on her trusted carpenter Justin Larot to come repair it, requiring complete discretion on his part. If he kept everything to himself, she promised to put him in her will. Justin Larot swore he would not say a word to anyone, and he kept that promise for many years. Henriette Launier did not forget him and did indeed include him in her will.

Henriette Launier then doubled down on her efforts to control Blanche. She had to find a way to break the girl's spirit so that she would stop trying to leave the house. Each time Blanche would fly into a rage, screaming about being held captive, Henriette Launier would crack down. She had heard Dr. Bauché talk about how they used ice-cold showers on violent mentally ill people at the hospital. She had made a mental note of it. Because they didn't have a shower, she began to use ice-cold baths on Blanche.

Blanche was terrorized by these baths, and several people were needed to force her into the bathtub. It took everything they had for Émilie Frasié, Marie Pinaud, and Henriette Launier to drag her to the tub. The thing that worked best was when they pulled her by the hair. It hurt so much that she complied.

The maids would spend twenty minutes fetching buckets of water from the well in the garden to fill the tub. As it was January when this all started, the water was freezing. Her mother would yell through the door that this was her punishment for throwing a fit: "I am telling you now, you will obey me!" When Blanche heard the maids carrying up the buckets of water, she knew what was in store for her. She would wrap her arms around the bedpost with all of her might. The maids would mutter swearwords as they climbed the stairs with the heavy full buckets. Clutching her bed, hearing them stomping up and down, Blanche would curse them too.

Once the bathtub was full of icy cold water, Marie Pinaud, Émilie Frasié, and Henriette Launier would start smacking Blanche's hands to make her let go of the bedpost. Then, with a maid on each side grabbing her arms, they would drag her across to bathroom where the tub was filled with icy water. Blanche would scream and resist as best she could, but the three women outnumbered her and would dunk her into the bath despite her tears and cries. To make sure she understood, her mother would force her head under the water for a few seconds. Blanche would feel the cold slowing her body and grow weak, going into shock. Her hands would turn blue and her face a pale gray. Her torturers would not notice, holding her in the bath.

They would keep her there for a full half hour, clocking it on a watch. "It shouldn't be too quick," Henriette Launier commanded, "she needs to remember this." The maids concurred, "This must put a stop to her antics so we can have some peace and quiet." Yes, Blanche needed to learn a lesson.

When it was finally over, they'd pull her out of the tub, for she'd no longer have the strength to lift herself up. They would lead her, naked, back to her room. No one would give her a towel to dry off or clothes to put on. They would just leave her there on her bed, half dead.

It would take Blanche a moment to realize that the ordeal was over and that she needed to get under a blanket to warm up. She'd pull the covers up and curl up underneath them, freezing. Her hands would turn an awful red color, her nails purple, and her skin burned. To stop the pain, she would scratch herself, muttering, "God, why have you abandoned me?" She would also call on her grandmother, but speaking softly so that it wouldn't happen again… She knew they could do it again any time they wanted, for they already had. She would pick up the rosary beads that hung on her bedpost and squeeze them tightly in her hands.

December 1884

Honoré Launier lived almost directly across the street from his mother and sister. He tried several times to have them over for lunch on a Sunday, but Henriette Launier always refused. His wife, Maria-Teresa, had also invited Blanche to go for a walk with her on several occasions, but her mother-in-law would never agree to it. Besides, Henriette Launier disliked her daughter-in-law and her granddaughter too for that matter. She found Dolorès to be a noisy, nosy, and ill-mannered child.

So, Honoré Launier took it upon himself to go upstairs and see his sister in her room. She poured out her heart to him. Fully aware that his sister's condition had been caused by a broken heart, he decided to have a few words with his mother about it.

"Why not let them marry? Gilles Lomet is a Républicain, yes, and the prefect is a Républicain as well. It's time to let them be together. If Blanche marries him, she'll get better and I just might get a better job at the prefecture."

"What right do you have to stick your nose into our business? Get out!"

Honoré Launier was sent away, but he was a good-natured fellow. His mother's attitude didn't really bother him. He came back over regularly and knocked on the door regularly, though for months no one answered it. Finally, one day, he was let back in.

Again, he went up to visit his sister in her room. That day, she had just come out of an ice bath and was deathly pale, clinging in fear to the side of her bed. He did love his sister, and seeing her like this, so fragile and so upset, he went off on his mother.

"What is going on with these ice baths? Have you lost your mind? Do you want to kill her?"

"You understand nothing of what goes on in this household. Get out! I never want to see your face here again. Stay out of our business or I'll cut off your allowance!"

Honoré Launier left the house. As soon as he got home, he decided he could not hold back anymore. He had to tell his mother how he felt. So, he sat down to write two letters, one to his mother and one to his sister. In the letter to his mother, he took his sister's side. On his last visit, he wrote, it was obvious to him how ill his sister was and that she needed to be taken to the hospital. He insisted on it and wrote at length about the duty he had to get her the help she needed. It was exactly the type of letter to push Henriette Launier over the edge.

In the letter to his sister, he encouraged her to do a little exercise, to get out of bed, to go down to the garden, to eat. He offered to take her for short walks on nice days, along with his wife, in Blossac Park, so that she could regain her strength and her appetite. Needless to say, this letter was read by Henriette Launier, and it only increased the anger she felt towards her son.

Naively, Honoré Launier thought that his mother had understood the seriousness of his message, and he showed up at 21 Rue de la Visitation with his wife and young daughter the following Sunday. Marie Pinaud slammed the door in their faces.

December 20, 1885

Dear Mother,

You sent me a letter full of nasty comments about me and my wife Maria-Teresa. But despite what you believe, my wife has only ever had kind words to say about you. She is raising our daughter Dolorès to love her family and to respect her grandmother. Yet, you never want to see our daughter. Why not? Why do you hate us so much? What have we done to make you so angry?

You say that you know Blanche best and that you are the only one who knows what's good for her. May I remind you that I am her brother and that I have my own opinions? When I tell you that Blanche is sick, I'm not criticizing you. There's no need for you to get so upset. I'm sure you are doing your best to care for her, but at a certain point, a mother's love is not enough. You need to know when to let go.

Blanche needs professional help. Open your eyes, Mother, don't you see how extremely thin Blanche is? I am not accusing you of anything. I am simply saying that Blanche cannot get the care she needs at home. No matter what you say, it's clear that she is sick, in fact, very sick. Keeping her at home is only making things worse. She needs to go to the Hôtel-Dieu as soon as possible. Do you want her to die? I'm sure you don't. Well, if you keep her at home without medical care, that's what will happen. Face the facts!

Please know that I am not questioning your ability to care for Blanche, but this is beyond what a mother can do. There's no shame in admitting that. And, again, I'm not criticizing you. I'm just saying that Blanche is not well, as you yourself have said many times, and that it has become a serious illness. Bring her to a doctor, for Pete's sake, and he will tell you the same thing.

Think about the consequences you may face if you keep her there; you could be accused of harming her and being a bad mother, which I know you're not. I know that you love Blanche, but your love is blind. You want her to be happy, so prove it. Send her to the hospital!

This is not the time to argue, Mother. I love you, and so does my wife, and my little Dolorès too. Don't get so upset just because someone disagrees with you. You love Blanche as only a mother can, so prove it. Send her to the hospital just for a few days, so that they can examine her, find out what's wrong, and help her to get better. Let the medical professionals handle it. They know what to do for her. You are not a doctor, so let the doctors do their job. They have experience with these kinds of illnesses.

Please, Mother, let your guard down and listen to your heart. Call for a coach and have Blanche taken to the hospital before Christmas.

Three times you've had Marie Pinaud slam the door in my face, even though my intentions were pure. Christmas is almost here. Isn't it time to put an end to all these quarrels and make peace with each other?

Please know that we love you. Give Blanche a kiss for us.

Your son,

Honoré

∾

Last Will and Testament dated January 5, 1885

Honoré never received a response to his letter and when he arrived at his mother's house on Christmas with his wife and daughter, no one opened the door. Henriette Launier hadn't even opened the letter yet. She was waiting until the new year to do so because she had a feeling that her son was going to ask her to do something and that it would be unpleasant.

When she finally did read the letter, she pursed her lips, a sign that meant her son had infuriated her yet again. This was not the first time he had sent a letter requesting medical care for Blanche, but this time he had really insisted, and she felt he had gone too far. So far, in fact, that she decided to disinherit him, to the extent allowed by law.

That's when she rewrote her last will and testament, reallocating her estate so as to ensure that she would go to heaven. She had no interest in the fiery flames of hell.

This is my last will and testament.

I, Henriette de Marcillat, widow of Dean Martin Launier, bequeath my estate as follows:

I leave to the Hospice of Poitiers a sum of fifteen hundred francs with the request that three hundred and sixty-five masses be said for me in my parish at Saint-Porchaire Church.

The Hospice shall also dedicate the same number of masses to my daughter Blanche upon her death.

I give and bequeath:

1. To Modeste Poineu, Émilie Frasié's sister, wife of François Firnaud, employee of the railroad, residing on Route de Biard in Poitiers, along with her aforementioned husband, the sum of twelve thousand francs.

2. To Louise Poineu, sister of Émilie Frasié, wife of Justin Larot, carpenter, residing on the Route de Bordeaux in Faubourg de la Tranche, the sum of twelve thousand francs.

3. To Madame Ferret, whose husband was principal of the Royal Academy and who resides in the village of Saint-Benoît, the sum of fifteen thousand francs, subject to usufruct. I give ownership of these funds to Madame Ferret's three daughters: Hélène, Marguerite, and Henriette.

4. To Alexandre Poineu, the godson of my daughter Blanche, a café waiter residing on Rue des Trois-Piliers in Poitiers, and to his wife Olympe, the sum of thirty thousand francs with the stipulation that they provide an annual allo-

wance of three hundred francs to Émilie Frasié and her husband Pierre Frasié for as long as they live, starting upon my death, but on condition that they are still in my employ at the time of my death. I give and bequeath this lifetime annuity to the Frasié couple only if the condition stipulated above is met.

If any of the beneficiaries listed above precede me in death and have descendants, it is my wish that their descendants receive the inheritance above, making them the beneficiaries in lieu of the individuals indicated above whom they represent.

I give and bequeath to the Hospice of Poitiers the sum of fifteen thousand francs, for them to maintain my tombstone in good condition in perpetuity, along with the tombstone of my husband Martin, who preceded me in death, and those of my relatives whose remains are in the family mausoleum that I had built in Chilvert and in which I wish to be buried, along with my daughter Blanche.

I do not want any other mausoleum to be built on the plot of land that I own, and I charge the Hospice of Poitiers and my executor hereafter named with this supervision and exclude this land from my estate.

To my daughter, Blanche Launier, should she outlive me, I give and bequeath by preciput and in addition to her share, for the duration of her life, the usufruct and enjoyment of the room she is currently living in, the room she lived in previously, and the one across from that and from my father's study, all located on the third floor of the house I currently reside in on Rue de la Visitation.

After my death, I want my daughter to continue to live in the part of the house I just described. She will be cared for by Émilie Frasié, to whom she is accustomed, and one or two Bons-Secours nuns whose motherhouse is in Blois.

If Émilie Frasié does not stay to care for my daughter after my death, the annual allowance described above shall not be paid to her.

All of my daughter's money, and any that she receives after my death, shall be used exclusively for her care.

Because my daughter is not capable of making decisions for herself or managing her money, I name Monsieur Durois, an attorney living in Poitiers, or if he is deceased, Maître Mireil, a lawyer in Poitiers, or Maître Fournieu, of Rue du Moulin-à-Vent in Poitiers, as her guardian and administrator of her estate. He shall also be charged with the full and complete execution of all of my arrangements and shall serve as the executor of my will.

To whichever of these attorneys accepts the difficult and delicate mission that I entrust to him, in recognition of his service, I give and bequeath the sum of five thousand francs. It is a small reward for all of the efforts he will expend in carrying out my wishes.

In the name of charity, I give and bequeath to the Petites Soeurs des Pauvres a sum of four thousand francs, and to the Bureau de Bienfaisance of this city a sum of one thousand francs.

The priest of the Saint-Porchaire parish shall distribute two hundred francs to the poor: I give him this sum for that purpose.

I do not believe that the aforementioned bequests exceed the value of the estate I am entitled to dispose of, but if this is the case, all of the bequests in cash except for those to the executor of my will, the Hospice, the Petites Soeurs des Pauvres, the Bureau de Bienfaisance, and the poor, shall each be reduced proportionally.

Should any of my heirs contest or refuse to execute my will, they shall be deprived of their share of my estate which, in that case only, shall instead be given to the Hospice of Poitiers.

All costs and expenses resulting from the bequests I have made shall be borne in full by my estate and paid by it.

I revoke all other previous wills.

I ask my beneficiaries to think of me sometimes and not to forget me in their prayers.

Will made in Poitiers, in my home on Rue de la Visitation, on the fifth of January, in the year eighteen hundred and eighty-five.

Henriette de Marcillat, the widow Launier.

This last will and testament was written by me on two sheets of watermarked paper costing one franc and twenty centimes which I have initialed.

The Widow Launier

~

Poitiers, 1887

Public education for children aged six to thirteen had become free and compulsory on June 16, 1881. From that date forward, it became illegal for children under thirteen to work. And beginning in 1886, every city was required to have a primary school. Cities with more than five hundred residents, like Poitiers, had to have two schools: one for boys and one for girls.

New teachers arrived fresh from the country's Écoles Normales Supérieures, and elected officials from the

Républicain party went from one school to the next for opening celebrations. On January 3, 1887, the two primary schools in Poitiers were inaugurated. Micheline Cénard and Valentin Roumi were the two teachers assigned to this city. Neither had been raised in Poitiers; the girls' teacher was from Lyon, and the boys' teacher from Bordeaux. They were both die-hard Républicains. They came with lofty goals, as they had been instructed to do. And they knew that it would not be easy to teach in a staunchly Catholic region, like Poitou.

The girls' school was temporarily set up in an old wine storehouse that was no longer in use. The building was repainted, larger windows were installed, and the inevitable linden tree was planted in the courtyard. There were new school desks with inkwells that Micheline Cénard had filled that very morning after stoking the fire in the wood-burning stove at the center of the room. Math and reading books sat on the desks, awaiting the children.

The boys' school was new construction and built just like other city schools: a large building with a main classroom, attached to a small residence for the teacher, an upstairs room that could be a second classroom or a study, a large courtyard with outdoor facilities next to the lawn, a second small yard for the teacher, and a section with plants for students to learn gardening. Naturally, the classroom was set up just like the one in the girls' school, with a woodstove lit by Valentin Roumi burning brightly in the middle of the room. There was a pot of milk heating on the stove for the first arrivals who had to come from farther away.

Each school was decorated with garlands bearing the colors of the Republic: blue, white, and red. It was to be a momentous occasion for both schools, located just one street away from each other. And, in a way, it was. Everything was ready. The teachers and city officials were waiting for the pupils to arrive. The problem was that only three boys and one girl came to enroll in school. Catholic families had received clear instructions: no one should attend a school where God was not present. It would mean risking your soul or even going to hell. Who would dare send their children to a secular school? Parenting was never easy... Of course, there were also parents who were worried about their family's reputation. The teachers had been so harshly criticized that people started to believe they led immoral lives. What would they teach the children? What kind of example would they set? Many had decided to wait and see.

Those first teachers needed to draw on all of their patience, knowledge, and skills, not to mention to prove their abilities by having their first groups of students pass the national exams, before schoolchildren would begin to fill the seats in their classrooms. Until that time, the battle for public support raged on and rooms remained fairly empty.

Jacob Lomet was kind of naïve as a politician and had truly expected more students to enroll. There had been so few Républicains standing with him when he started out, and now he was surrounded by them. He was sure they would come. He gave a speech at each school that day. He started at the girls' school where the only listeners were the teacher, a young couple who were cobblers, and their ten-year-old daughter who had never before been to school. They insisted on being there for her first day. Two hours later, he spoke at the boys' school, where there were the sons of three workers from the print shop, their mothers, and the teacher Valentin Roumi.

At both locations, Jacob Lomet spoke about perseverance, the righteousness of their cause, and the ideals of Républicains, luring in the dreamy-eyed teachers with visions of a French Republic filled with educated citizens who were the product of a secular public school system. "Thanks to our public schools," he declared, "children will no longer go to work in the factories. Instead, they will experience the best moments of their lives learning from their teachers." He also promised to give prizes to students who received good marks.

As soon as he finished with his speeches, he went to order the most beautiful copies of books by Victor Hugo, Jean-Jacques Rousseau, and George Sand, with red leather covers and gilded edges. He purchased two copies of each, to be used as prizes awarded to the top students in math, spelling, and civics in each school. Afterwards, he would write to the Minister of Education recommending that these kinds of prizes be awarded in every school, which is indeed a custom that was widely adopted.

While his father was busy with the new schools, Gilles Lomet was dedicating his spare time to a Christian social organization that was trying to improve conditions for factory workers. He met with the group twice a week, Wednesday and Saturday evenings. It was run mostly by Catholics, but included a few Protestants from Poitiers as well. And it was socially diverse: there were intellectuals like Gilles Lomet and also working-class people. The organization had been created in 1884 and was one of four hundred such groups working throughout France.

Catholics felt it was part of their mission, if not their primary concern, to help the poor. They were aware of the conditions that factory workers endured and had decided to try to help those most in need. It was also a response to the anticlerical sentiment that had developed among working-class people. Originally, the majority of French Catholics thought it was their duty to be Royalists. They spent their time going from one procession to honor the Virgin Mary to the next, praying that the crime committed against France be undone: that it return to a monarchy. The next generation, however, changed course, bringing social classes together by either becoming Républicains or at least finding their place within the French Republic.

Albert de Mun, Léon Hamel, and René de la Tour du Pin were the leaders of the Catholic social organizations. They were all ardent supporters of the labor laws enacted in 1884 and 1889 that allowed for unionization, limited the workday to eleven hours, made child labor illegal, and protected those injured in work-related accidents.

Certainly, conservative Catholics were never fans of these new groups, but over time, they came to understand the problems workers faced in society. Industrialist Léon Hamel led the way for Catholic factory owners. He incorporated Catholic social doctrine into the design of his business in Val-des-Bois well before any others. As early as 1883, he had created a factory council comprised of both executives and factory workers.

René de la Tour du Pin, a forefather of this movement, believed and stated loud and clear that a just society must be built on a system of representation. He viewed the capitalist law of supply and demand as inequitable. There had to be a better way: a system where those profiting from the industry and those working in it had equal voices. De la Tour du Pin had been raised in Switzerland and descended from a long line of Protestants, and the values learned there were the catalyst for his new way of thinking. From 1884 to 1891, there were regular meetings held in Fribourg to debate these ideas, giving a European dimension to the movement happening in France.

With the blessing of Pope Leo XIII, these forward-thinking men would rally the Republic together behind them. Famous authors, the likes of Émile Zola, would support them. Zola's novels brought to light the deplorable conditions of workers in that era. His epic *Germinal*, to name just one book, portrayed the terrible realities of the lives of miners in the North.

Although Henriette Launier had no intention of allowing her daughter to live her own life and planned to keep her at home forever, she did still fear God. Every Saturday, she would go to confession. Behind the latticed confessional screen, she spoke of minor sins and Father Mallouet always gave her absolution. He thought Henriette Launier was like a saint. Plus, she always paid her contribution to the parish on time and gave more than a lot of the other bourgeois families. The priest had absolutely no complaints about her.

With her participation in Sunday morning mass, vespers, and evening prayers, along with saying the rosary, Henriette Launier proved herself to be an upstanding woman in the parish. She was often held up as an example for others, and Father Mallouet liked her and felt comfortable around her. So, when he noticed that Blanche was no longer attending mass, he decided to ask her mother about it.

"My poor daughter is not the same since her grandfather passed away. She never wants to go out anymore and doesn't like visitors."

"She knows me quite well. I'm sure she'd want to see me."

"Oh, Father, I don't think so. When anyone enters her room, she starts to scream."

"Has she lost her reason?"

"No, but she just doesn't want to see anyone. And she has terrible asthma attacks when she gets upset."

"Let me speak to her. I know she'll be happy to see me."

"Please be patient, Father, not just yet...maybe when she is feeling better."

They went around and around, the conversation ending with a "no, thank you." Then, one night, Father Mallouet died, as sometimes happens to ninety-three-year-old men, after falling into a deep sleep. Father Potier became the head priest at Saint-Porchaire. Henriette Launier didn't know him well. She had crossed paths with him at some point, but they had never spoken. She had never even heard him celebrate a mass because she always went to the older priest's masses.

On more than one occasion, Father Mallouet had spoken to his colleague about his concerns regarding Blanche and about her mother's refusal to let him see her. The new priest was young and dynamic, and he didn't buy any of Henriette Launier's excuses. He started to express his surprise that Blanche no longer came to mass. Every time he would see Henriette Launier, he'd ask her about it. He was shocked that the daughter of one of the church's most prominent parishioners no longer attended mass and had not taken communion in years.

Henriette Launier disliked the new priest and considered his interrogations to be harassment. When she was unable to avoid him, she would respond evasively. This did not deter the young priest, who insisted that he visit Blanche, as he did all of the sick of the parish, explaining that it was his duty to comfort her.

One Saturday, he was the only priest hearing confession, so Henriette Launier could not avoid him by choosing another. Just before she confessed, he spoke to her.

"I'm going to see Blanche this afternoon."

"She doesn't want any visitors."

"But she'll agree to see me. Anyway, it's my duty to speak to her."

"I assure you that she has everything she needs. She wants for nothing."

"I'm going, and I will hear her confession."

"Her confession? What for?"

"Do not forget, Madame Launier, that if she dies without having confessed her sins, she will go to Hell and it will be because of you and your obstinance in refusing to let us see her. And you will go to Hell as well."

To avoid the eternal inferno, Henriette Launier agreed to receive the priest in her home at three o'clock, but she took precautions to prepare her daughter for it.

"Our parish priest is coming to see you to hear your confession and give you communion."

"I'm not dying. Why would he want to come see me?"

"It's been years since you've attended mass. Don't forget that you're the one who decided not to go to church, and make sure you tell him that. It's not my fault if you never want to leave your room."

"I have nothing to say to him. Tell him not to come."

"He is going to come, and you will not start telling tales, as you've been known to do in the past."

"Fine. Let old Father Mallouet come see me."

"*Quelle imbécile!* Father Mallouet is dead. It's his replacement, Father Potier, who is coming to see you. And I'm telling you again, you will not start up with your foolishness."

"What am I supposed to tell him? Nothing ever happens here."

"You know what I'm talking about, all of your ridiculous complaints that have caused me so much pain."

Blanche was silent. She was trying to figure out if she should send the priest away or welcome him with open arms. As her mother spoke, she wondered if God himself was sending this priest to her.

"If you speak one word of your crazy ideas, Blanche, you will have an ice bath every day for a month! You hear me? Every day!"

Blanche's lips trembled. She knew full well what her mother was capable of. She let out a timid *"Oui"* to show her mother that she understood. But her mother had little faith in her daughter and decided to take preventive measures. One hour before the priest's arrival, she had buckets of water brought up from the well, and Blanche was forced to get in. This time, though, they washed her with soap, her mother muttering: "What would people think about me if you were to greet someone looking like the dirty slob that you normally are?" Adding: "You see how cold this water is, so pay attention to what you say to the priest or you'll be having an icy bath like this every day."

One of the maids suggested that they could have warmed up the water since Blanche was not having one of her nervous breakdowns and there was no reason for it to be so unbearably cold. Henriette Launier did not take the suggestion well and fired her. Meanwhile, Émilie Frasié put a clean shirt on Blanche and started to comb her hair. It had been so long since she had combed it and there were so many knots in her hair that Blanche started to cry from the pain. They put fresh sheets on her bed and pillowcases scented with lavender. The room was cleaned up, and Henriette Launier put a pretty bouquet of sweet-smelling roses on the nightstand next to Blanche's bed.

So, when Father Potier entered the room, he found a sick young woman, very pale for sure, but otherwise quite decent, all dressed up in an impeccably clean room. Blanche tried to smile, but still in shock from the ice bath, she just shivered nervously.

Honoré Launier had contended that his sister was ill and needed medical attention. He said in his letter that Blanche was dying and questioned if his mother was going to just let her die. Henriette Launier kept saying that she wasn't so sick that she might die, and she believed it. According to her, Blanche was only confined to her room because she was possessed. Henriette had spoken to Father Potier about this, but after his visit with Blanche, he made it quite clear that he did not believe that to be the case. What Blanche needed was a husband and some children. A woman who is baptized and does not become a nun has the duty to marry. It's God's will:

go forth and multiply! That is what she has been called to do.

Blanche had, in fact, confided in the priest. She told him that she was in love with Gilles Lomet and that she couldn't live without him. But Father Potier advised her not to disobey her mother and to marry someone else. He offered to introduce her to one of his parishioners who was an expert at finding suitable husbands for young ladies. Her matchmaking skills had resulted in more than one wedding in the parish and, as the priest put it, the couples were no more and no less happy than any others. And these marriages produced beautiful babies that he joyfully baptized in his church.

Just the thought of Blanche getting married was intolerable for Henriette Launier, so she fiercely opposed the idea. To tell the truth, it wasn't just that she opposed Blanche's marriage to Gilles Lomet, her family's nemesis that she wanted nothing to do with. No, it didn't matter who the future son-in-law might be. She wanted nothing to do with any of it. Henriette Launier thus decided that Father Potier was a dangerous man and that she had to do everything in her power to stop him from coming to her house. The next time the priest announced that he was planning to come see Blanche again to give her communion, she told him that after his last visit Blanche had such a terrible asthma attack that she almost died of asphyxiation. Fearing for her life, the doctor had ordered that she not receive any more visitors. That said, she added, "Please pray for her soul, Father." And she paid for a mass to be said for her daughter's health. After that, any time Father Potier broached the subject, she'd just refuse and give him money to have a mass dedicated to her.

This wasn't easy for her, because she was extraordinarily miserly, and that in fact was the main reason why she didn't want her daughter to marry. She was worried about losing her wealth. Marriages cost money: a dowry. Not to mention that a husband might start sticking his nose in her affairs and find out that Blanche had received a large inheritance. It could very well be that Blanche might take her to court. No need to risk any of that.

Henriette Launier really didn't believe that her daughter was sick. In her mind, Blanche was possessed. What else, after all these years, could be causing her obsession with that lawyer? That monster who was against the Catholic Church, who hated the Pope, who supported secular schooling, who must in some way be in cahoots with Satan...? Whenever Blanche spoke about Gilles Lomet, she sounded like she had just seen him the other day. All this time, and she had not forgotten a thing about him. This lovesickness could be nothing other than possession. Yes, he had possessed her soul with this demonic love, and it needed to be extracted from her heart.

How to rid her daughter of this possession was all Henriette Launier could think about. Saint Radegonde, whose relics were in the church in Poitiers bearing her name, was known to help with exorcisms. But how could she convince Blanche to go there? Blanche would have to admit that she was possessed, and that wouldn't be easy.

For a while, Henriette Launier would go up to her daughter's room every afternoon at a time she thought Blanche might be open to chatting with her. She would obstinately try to convince her to come along to pray to Saint Radegonde so that she might be released from the hold of the devil incarnated in Gilles Lomet. Their conversations would inevitably end in a quarrel, with Blanche arguing that Gilles Lomet believed in Christ just like her, that he had nothing to do with the devil, and that their love had nothing to do with being possessed. After a week of fruitless attempts, Henriette Launier concluded that she would have to do this another way.

Marie Pinaud was originally from Loudun, where all the nuns in one convent were famously possessed in 1634. With her help, Henriette Launier was able to locate an elderly monk living in that town who was known to have performed exorcisms on numerous people possessed by the devil and had a fairly high success rate. She sent for him straight away. He arrived with three young monks during the Advent season before Christmas. He was very thin, had a fixed gaze, rarely blinked, and his eyes sparkled. He wore a monk's habit and Roman sandals with bare feet, even though it was snowing out. The monks who accompanied him were dressed the same way, but were carrying bags, ropes, and boxwood branches.

The moment she laid eyes on them, Blanche knew she was in danger. Her mother tried to say something, but the monks hurried her out of the room. Blanche didn't have time to ask what was happening before the monks started grabbing her wrists and ankles, holding her down on the bed with her arms and legs spread out. Blanche screamed as they tied her to the bed in that position. She tried to defend herself, but the monks overpowered her. She yelled for help as loud as she could, but no one came.

Without hitting her too hard, the old monk rhythmically touched her head and feet with the boxwood branches, saying phrases that were incomprehensible, maybe speaking Greek. Blanche was completely terrorized and looked at him with wild bulging eyes. Finally, he started speaking words she could understand: "Unholy spirit, leave this body! Devil Gilles, leave this woman!" Then, he asked her: "Do you fear God? Do you fear his Holy Name?" Blanche, trembling in fear, remained mute. The monk continued: "Holy Spirit, dispel the shadows hiding the ugliness and malice of her sins." The younger monks started slowly striking her with whips, while the older one continued to speak: "Make her understand how horrendous sins are, dear God, so that she learns to hate all sins and to hate the one who has led her into such depravity. Tell me, Blanche, who was baptized at birth, do you hate all sins? Respond!" Blanche's teeth were chattering and her body was convulsing, despite the ropes attaching her to the bed. The monk persisted: "Here she is, Lord, full of confusion and overcome with the pain of her mistakes. In a loud voice, repeat after me: I renounce all sins and sinners, and I will no longer make any pacts with the devil Gilles. Do you renounce the devil Gilles? Answer, you hear me, answer!" The monks continued their lashes... "Repeat after me, or you will lose your skin: I believe in one God..." The monks were still whipping... "the Father, the Almighty, Creator of Heaven and Earth, and in his only Son Jesus Christ, our Lord..." Overcome with fear, Blanche repeated the words as best she could, losing consciousness as she pronounced the words of the Apostles' Creed.

The old monk was still bellowing: "Repeat after me: I confess to God Almighty, to the Holy Virgin Mary, to Saint Michael the Archangel, to Saint John the Baptist, to the Apostles Saint Peter and Saint Paul, to all the saints, that I have greatly sinned through my thoughts and in my words, in what I have done, and in what I have failed to do; through my fault, through my fault, through my most grievous fault."

The monks stopped hitting her, but she could see something terrible in their faces. Paralyzed, Blanche waited for what was to come next. The old monk was not done yet:

"Cure her, Lord, for evil has penetrated deep into the marrow of her bones. Because she was silent and failed to confess her crimes, her body is failing her and she is screaming in agony." A more violent thrashing of the whip made her yell out in pain. The monk continued: "My wounds are tainted and festering because of my sins. Jesus, whose side was pierced by a lance..." Blanche felt a stab in her left side.

"Jesus shed blood and water..." They cut her hands so they were bleeding. Blanche wailed...

"His hands and feet were pierced by nails. The crowd spat on him and threw dirt in his wounds."

The four monks spat on Blanche's face.

"A crown of thorns..."

They thrust a crown of spikey bramble on her head, scratching her face and scalp. Blood dripped from the wounds.

When the exorcism was over, after the monks untied her and left the room, Blanche curled up in a fetal position. After all of the years of isolation, this experience pushed her to the edge of insanity. In an awful state of shock, she felt as if she were losing her mind.

VIII

1891

The Panama Canal scandal was at its peak. The great Ferdinand de Lesseps, the engineer of the Suez Canal, had failed. He had estimated the cost of construction at 600 million francs, but it was nearing double that amount! This Panama Canal project was a money pit and was also costing the lives of workers who were dying on the job site. The company funding it had already lost 1,400 million francs and the work was only half done. The company had been liquidated on February 4, 1889, although the small private investors were not immediately made aware of this. Thanks to a number of obscure protections set in place, it took more than three years for the bankruptcy to come to light.

The scandal rocked all of France and rattled public opinion. Politicians who were previously considered to possess a high level of integrity now appeared to have taken bribes to deceive investors and lure them into investing in the project despite the risks involved. A parliamentary commission was formed and its investigation led to the arrest of the company's directors and the indictment of the minister of public works, Charles Baïhaut. Other prominent Républicains appeared to be linked to this dirty business.

Maître Jacob Lomet had had blind faith in the project and had invested all of his savings in the Panama Canal. Like the other 25,000 French citizens involved, he lost everything. On top of losing his entire life savings, the old lawyer had the sad realization that Républicain elected officials could be corrupted and were capable of dragging people into ruin. At the age of eighty-seven, he not only lost his family's fortune but his faith in the political system, everything he had worked for his whole life. It was a fall from grace that he would never recover from.

Everyone who had invested, old and young alike, came to him demanding to be refunded their investments. They reminded him that he had been the one to lead them into this scheme through his unwavering support for Ferdinand de Lesseps and the shady bankers he colluded with. A long line of suddenly impoverished men marched through his living room, and Jacob Lomet, his shoulders hunched, tried to give them the courage to go on... After a whole week of such visits, in front of a group of his old friends who were explaining that they had lost everything because of him and that they were going to demand that his house be seized, he did not have the strength to keep going. He had a heart attack and died right in front of them.

He was buried two days later, but few people attended the funeral. His reputation had been forever damaged by the Panama Canal scandal.

Gilles Lomet lost both of his parents that year, his mother dying just one week after his father. Rachel Lomet was also quite old when she passed away at the age of eighty-one. She had contracted a severe case of whooping cough and died of asphyxia. Knowing that her husband had lost everything and had contributed to the financial ruin of their friends had been one of the major factors in her declining health. She had always been an unwavering supporter of her husband, and so she departed with him.

Maître Gilles Lomet had no brothers or sisters and found himself alone at the age of fifty-three. Although he had stopped seeing Blanche years ago, he had never forgotten her, and his parents' deaths reminded him of that cruel loss. He had always kept tabs on the Launier family, from a distance. He learned that Blanche had never married, despite what the maid had told him. He had heard the gossip that she was not well, although no one could explain exactly what illness she had. He also knew that her father and grandfather had died and that Blanche and her mother were the only two living at 21 Rue de la Visitation. He was aware, of course, that Blanche's mother had a reputation of being ultra-Catholic, more of a Royalist than the royal family themselves, and more fiercely anti-Républicain than her husband had been, if such a thing were possible.

Whenever he thought about why it didn't work out with Blanche, he would look at it from every angle possible and always land on the same conclusion: her parents had forced her to break it off with him because he was a Républicain and maybe also because he was Protestant... And now that Républicains were being disparaged, he felt sad and ashamed that he had lost the only woman he had ever loved just because of politics. He felt quite old.

Even before the whole kerfuffle with the Panama Canal, he had started to step back from politics, in particular from the Républicains, despite his affection for his parents. After the scandal broke, he instead dove further into his work on social issues. He moved out of the apartment he had moved into when he started dating Blanche, the place where they had all of their romantic *rendezvous*, and moved back into his parents' stately mansion which, luckily, had never been mortgaged. There, he opened up a pro bono legal aid office, open every afternoon from 5pm to 8pm, even on Saturdays and Sundays. Everyone who had fallen victim to Ferdinand de Lesseps' scam came seeking his advice. How to help those who had been so shamefully deceived, that was what kept him busy.

He went to court for them, without charging any fees. He tried and lost his cases, one after the other. The judges so rarely sided against the audacious financiers Cornelius Herz and the Baron de Reinach, that the public became outraged. Two out of every three cases were appealed by the defendants and overturned on the grounds of procedural irregularities. This was the dirtiest affair Gilles Lomet had ever dealt with in court, and he had his hands full.

Luckily, a major event occurred that would take his mind off of these cases and give him the courage he needed to continue on: Pope Leo XIII published the encyclical Rerum Novarum on May 15, 1891. The Pope had heard the appeals made by the workers' organization he was involved with. For the first time ever, the Catholic Church's highest authority was tackling the issues of the working class. This encyclical letter brought Gilles Lomet even closer to his Catholic comrades. Any lingering traces of anti-papal sentiment he might have been holding on to were forever erased.

The Rerum Novarum encyclical was a veritable revolution in the Catholic world. The letter spoke of the need to reject the inevitability of class struggle, a point upon which all Catholics agreed, but it added that capitalism in its current form should be rejected, that there should be open dialogue with workers, that their deplorable working conditions needed to be improved. That was radical thinking. This encyclical paved the way for social Catholicism. From that moment on, all Catholic factory owners had to change the way they ran their businesses or risk failing to be good Christians.

After his legal aid consultations on Saturday nights, Gilles Lomet would host the workers' organization meetings in his home. He also actively contributed to the group's magazine, *Sillon*. It had just started to be published and was so successful and so widely distributed by the group's members that people no longer called it the workers' organization, they called it the Sillon group. The magazine published interesting articles by Marc Sangnier, one of the group's Catholic leaders who wrote about the encyclical Rerum Novarum. The Sillon group wanted to see the encyclical's tenets put into practice, hoping to incorporate Christian values into the workplace. With the increase in anarchist attacks in France, the steps Christian groups were taking seemed to be a revolutionary and constructive alternative. Young graduates of the country's most prestigious Écoles Normales and Écoles Polytechniques joined forces with the Sillon group to fight for a more just society.

Ever since the traumatic visit of the four monks, Blanche lived in fear that they might come back again. She spent hours lying in bed, in a stupor, listening to every little sound and imagining the worst, terrified by the sound of any voice she didn't recognize... She was sleeping less and less. When she was able to fall asleep, she would wake up late in the morning and gobble down a chocolate-filled croissant, but then wouldn't eat at all at noon. Sometimes she got hungry at night, and they would bring her brioche, if they remembered to. She never asked for anything for herself.

After the exorcism, Blanche stopped yelling and throwing fits. She was so petrified that when she felt herself growing angry about being locked up or about being abused, she would bite her sheets so that she would not make a sound. Eventually, Émilie Frasié noticed the holes in the sheets and reported it to Henriette Launier, who coolly responded: "If that's how things are, then she will have no more sheets on the bed."

Blanche became very weak and visibly emaciated. Her eyes were so sunken and her cheeks so hollow that one of the maids who had brought water up to her, Constance Dupuis, felt the need to mention it to Henriette Launier. She was fired on the spot. The household became a revolving door for maids; most lasted fewer than two months! The most faithful stayed, of course: Émilie Frasié and Marie Pinaud.

Henriette wanted to silence her daughter but not to kill her. So, the ice baths were discontinued. All baths, for that matter. Blanche never asked to take a bath, so they didn't bathe her. She sunk down deeper and deeper in her filth. She grew fingernails that were five centimeters long and pitch black. Her hair, which was never cut, was impressively long, falling below her waist, but matted from never being combed and infested with lice. It all made her look quite hideous.

Completely helpless, Blanche never said a word. Sometimes she would mutter, "Queen of the Heavens, save me, have pity on me." Sometimes she would write on the walls. But the moment she would hear someone coming up the stairs, she would quickly launch herself onto the bedpost and squeeze her eyes shut in terror.

One morning at dawn, after not sleeping a wink, she was listening to the sounds in the street below. Street cleaners were out on Rue de la Visitation. They were cleaning the paved street with buckets of water and large brooms, brushing away debris. As she listened to them work, she invented stories in her mind. One of the street cleaners was going to bash open the shutters on her window, breaking them to pieces with a shovel, and she would fly out towards the sky like a swallow who had been nesting on the windowsill, breaking free of the darkness and the impenetrable shuttered window.

At nine o'clock, the postman swiftly made his way down the street and stopped in front of the prison, as usual...

Eleven o'clock, a knife-sharpener passed by with his cart.

On a good day, around five o'clock the barrel organ would pull up and play a sad song under her window. The organist would sing, and Blanche would cry, softly.

The Paris-Toulouse train whistle would sound at six o'clock. Another train would pass through after without stopping.

The stiflingly hot summer air would enter the room through the small dormer. There was going to be a thunderstorm... Blanche would feel a bowel movement coming. Why bother getting up? With her eyes tightly shut, she would relieve herself in the bed. Why bother living?

June 1894

"À bas l'anarchie!"

"Down with anarchy! Where are the police? Death to the anarchists!"

All of France was enraged, and in Poitiers, like everywhere else, crowds were gathering. The streets leading to Place d'Armes were swarmed with people. Sadi Carnot, the President of the French Republic, had just been assassinated!

Sadi Carnot knew some people in Poitiers, so his death was mourned even more there than elsewhere. Born and raised in Limoges, he still had a number of friends in the region and used to return often for visits. Two years earlier, he had come to Châtellerault to tour the weapons manufacturing factory. The tireless Sadi Carnot, the one who zigzagged the country from north to south and east to west to learn and listen and to try to solve problems in the provinces, the most popular president ever to take office, the leader who invited the mayors of every city in France to come to Paris for a grand banquet, this Sadi Carnot had just been assassinated by anarchists in Lyon.

In Poitiers, they were protesting against the wave of anarchy spreading across the country, striking the upper classes as often as the lower classes. A year ago, August Vaillant had thrown a bomb into the Chamber of Deputies. The anarchists were terrorists who wanted to destabilize the Republic, so they also hit public places: cafés, cinemas, theaters, stairways...and there were casualties. All of France was on edge because of them. Pushed into action by the death of Sadi Carnot, the French public took to the streets, demanding the government provide stricter enforcement and protect its people.

The terrorist attacks had started in 1892. A small handful of radicals—Ravachol, Henry, and Liabeuf—were rebelling against society and everyone was afraid. Originally a philosophical movement initiated by intellectuals like Élisée Reclus, Jean Grave, and Sébastien Faure, it had degenerated into terrorism. The agitators were not contained to any one area, so everyone was scared. Anarchy was spreading across Europe. The king of Italy, Umberto I, had just been the victim of a terrorist attack. He died during the second attempt on his life. Even the United States was scared and began to protest against the anarchy movement after it took the life of President McKinley.

In France, there was not a city that was spared this disquiet. There hadn't been such a large crowd gathered in Poitiers in ages. For the first time ever, Républicains and Royalists were protesting together. Henriette Launier, remembering the attack on Napoléon III, joined the throngs of people in the streets. A few steps away from her was Gilles Lomet, but they didn't recognize each other in the mob of people.

Henriette Launier rarely saw Blanche anymore. Émilie Frasié would bring some food up to Blanche every night at eight o'clock. Blanche no longer had the strength to get out of bed and had stopped using the chamber pot. There were no sheets on the mattress, just a piece of oilcloth spread out underneath her. No one bothered to bathe her anymore. She looked dreadful: haggard eyes that looked huge because she was so thin, a gaunt face, yellowish skin, and hair crawling with lice.

She did have an old blanket on top of her. Whenever she was frightened, she'd pull the crusty blanket up over her head and hide her face. She rarely complained, and never did so in the presence of her dreaded mother. Sometimes, when she was alone, she would mumble, but it would be an endless string of words and she would speak patois, like the servants did. Émilie Frasié, who still slept in her room, spoke a country patois.

One day, Henriette sent for a chimney sweep to come clean the fireplace in Blanche's room. She had wood brought in and made a pile of firewood in her daughter's room. She was attentive that day, and made sure that Émilie Frasié went up at regular intervals to add a log to the fire in Blanche's room. "She mustn't catch a cold," Henriette said. Obviously, if she got sick, her mother would have to bring in a doctor and a doctor might demand that Blanche be taken to the hospital.

Henriette Launier's son was like a stranger to her, and he couldn't possibly comprehend the issue. Blanche could only live at home. She was the one who chose to stay in her room; she liked it. They should leave her be. Although she would never admit that there was anything seriously wrong with Blanche, she also didn't want anyone to see her like that. She could not allow herself to see how completely unraveled Blanche had become.

Father Potier no longer requested to come visit Blanche, although he continued to ask about her. At least Henriette Launier didn't have to deal with that anymore. She had been living with her daughter for many years and knew exactly what she needed, in any case.

She went above and beyond and ordered oysters for Blanche one day, knowing how much she loved them. When the oysters were brought to her room, Blanche had one or two, but Émilie Frasié finished most of them. It was not the first time Henriette Launier had purchased oysters for her daughter. She did so every time she started to feel uncomfortable about the situation. But it was not uncommon for the maid to eat them, and Henriette Launier never checked to find out. There was no more dialogue between mother and daughter, so she wouldn't know whether Blanche was eating or not. She sometimes worried that Blanche might not be eating at all, but her conscience was clear. She was providing food and doing her duty as a mother, even if her daughter was as utterly ungrateful as her son.

∽

January 1898: The Dreyfus Affair

It had been three years since Captain Alfred Dreyfus had been convicted of treason. He was accused of communicating French military secrets to the Germans. Later, it was proven that these accusations were false and that Dreyfus had been charged with the crime because he was Jewish.

In early 1898, the Dreyfus Affair captivated the people of Poitiers, less so than in Paris, but it still divided the city into two camps. Unsurprisingly, it was the ultra-Catholics who were convinced of his guilt and the Républicains who were sure of his innocence.

Henriette Launier, now essentially cut off from society, was uninterested in the debate. For some time, she had lost all interest in the issues consuming her compatriots. Gilles Lomet, however, championed Captain Dreyfus, even if he was starting to slow down physically. The lawyer and his workers' group were great admirers of the author Émile Zola, who had so poignantly captured the details of the daily struggles of the working class in his novels. So, when Zola's legendary article *"J'accuse!"* came out in *Aurore*, defending Dreyfus against his detractors, they all pored over it.

Everyone agreed with Gilles Lomet that they should denounce the antisemitism that had motivated Dreyfus' enemies. Zola's famous article was on display in his office. The workers' organization of Poitiers even published a short piece in *L'Avenir de la Vienne* to express their solidarity with Captain Dreyfus.

⌇

1899

Gilles Lomet was dead.

Henriette Launier read it in the newspaper and bounded up the staircase two steps at a time to wave it in front of Blanche's face. Mute, buried in a dark melancholy, did she even remember Gilles Lomet, the man she had once loved so much? There was no response, not a muscle moved when she heard the news.

For once, Henriette Launier was telling the truth. Gilles Lomet was really dead. This moment, one she had stopped holding out hope for, had actually arrived. That cursed lawyer could no longer bother her daughter. She now had absolutely nothing left to fear.

Gilles Lomet died of pleurisy at the age of sixty-one. He had not outlived his parents by very many years. He also didn't die suddenly. He had battled pneumonia in the spring for quite a long time, and it had worn him down. He even had to go to the hospital, but after a week, knowing that the end was near, he asked to return home. He died in his bed after suffering in agony for over twenty-four hours. His Sillon friends took turns at his bedside. They were the ones who called for his pastor to come be with him during his final moments.

Gilles Lomet had no descendants, as he had never married. He had no brothers or sisters, and his aunts and uncles had already passed on. He left most of his estate to support the social work done by his parish and thirty thousand francs to fund the publication of *Sillon*.

Unlike his parents' funerals, which were sparsely attended, many people showed up to say goodbye to Gilles Lomet, including all of his friends from the Christian workers' group that now numbered over one hundred members. In Poitiers, there had never been a Protestant funeral attended by so many Catholics.

No one paid any attention to the little old lady dressed in black who was watching from afar. It was Henriette Launier. She didn't dare enter the Protestant church, for she would never set foot in a place that wasn't Catholic, but she couldn't help herself from going to the cemetery. It was beyond her control. She had to see with her own eyes that Gilles Lomet, the horrid monster who had ruined her life and her daughter's as well, was really dead. She watched as they lowered the casket into the ground, and after everyone had left, she got closer to read the headstone. Gilles Lomet had been buried in the family plot. Henriette read the names of his parents engraved above his own name. She was overcome with an indescribable feeling of serenity. Her nightmare was finally over. She was about to go out through the cemetery gates when she changed her mind. She went back to read the headstone again, to reassure herself that what she had seen was actually true.

At last, she left. She was so happy and light on her feet that she walked the whole way back. Several times, she had to stop and place her hands on her chest because her heart was pounding. She finally arrived home. Once she settled in, she started to feel cold and asked for a fire to be lit in her fireplace and in her daughter's room as well. She was so abnormally cheerful that the maids started to think that she might be losing her mind too.

May 1901

In the span of just a few years, Henriette Launier had found a way to fire eight different maids. Any time one of them tried to say something about Blanche's condition, she'd be sent packing. Some lasted three months, others just a week. She had just fired another one, Bernadette Chaigneau, and Prudence Renou was taking her place. Prudence was eighteen, a pretty girl, sure of herself, and this was her first job.

To keep the peace, Henriette Launier had long ago relinquished care of her daughter to Émilie Frasié, who had continued to work for her. She was the one who slept in Blanche's room, ever since the infamous night when Blanche tried to escape out of the window. But, unfortunately for Henriette Launier, the maid was not immortal. Émilie Frasié passed away. This posed a problem for Henriette. Who would be assigned to stay with Blanche? She decided that no one would. In her present state, Blanche was no longer a flight risk. Prudence Renou was tasked with bringing food to her room.

When Prudence saw the state of Blanche's room, the catastrophically deplorable conditions she was living in, on a straw mattress crawling with bugs, with no sheets, lying in her own excrement, she went and told Henriette Launier that she was going to clean it all up. Henriette Launier objected forcefully, saying that if she didn't like it, she could take her leave.

This insufferable new maid, the death of Émilie Frasié, Henriette found all of this to be quite annoying. She kept to her room for several weeks, and the maid took advantage of that time to show others Blanche's room. In particular, she showed it to a deliveryman who, that night, wrote to the public prosecutor.

Monsieur,

I am writing on behalf of several outraged individuals to tell you about a very serious concern. At 21 Rue de la Visitation, there is an elderly woman named Launier who lives with a daughter who has been held captive there for 25 years. The window has been shuttered and locked closed, and for years, only one old maid was ever allowed to enter the room.

The poor thing is always kept naked and in a repugnant state of filth.

In the name of all that is humane, I beg you to use your powers to intercede on her behalf. If you refuse, I shall write to the Minister of Justice so that the old woman is charged with this crime and takes her turn sleeping in a locked room.

Signed,

A good citizen who is appalled

The prosecutor showed the letter to Commissioner Bucheton, head of the police force, who went to the home to see for himself what was going on. At first, Henriette Launier obstinately refused to allow them to enter. They also tried to speak with her son across the street, who did the same. The commissioner disregarded their wishes and forced his way into 21 Rue de la Visitation.

These were his first impressions when he saw Blanche's room, as recounted in *L'Avenir de la Vienne* on May 25:

"When the commissioner opened the door to the room, he could barely see anything because it was almost completely dark. A rancid smell, unidentifiable, unimaginable, hung in the air. The window was closed and the shutters nailed and locked shut. There was some rubble in a corner, and a dirty mattress. There, on an oil-cloth, he saw a human being who had been reduced to an animal. It was a woman, hiding under a blanket, muttering inarticulately. She was completely naked and was so thin that she looked like a skeleton. Her thighs were as big as a regular person's wrists, her arms as thin as the neck of a bottle, her fingers were like pencils but with extremely long fingernails at the tips. She was frightening to look at...her hair, left tangled for so many years, was in an odd braid that fell down past her hips, it was matted and looked waxy, crusted with filth, infested by generations of insects, with cockroaches crawling in and out.

"Around her bed, there was just waste. She was lying on a layer of grime, a dry paste formed by excrement, secretions, bits of meat and putrefied bread, built up over the years. In it, there were enormous worms wriggling about, rats, and all sorts of vermin.

"There were even worms living in the captive woman's skin."

The prosecutor was called to the scene. He ordered Blanche to be transported to the Hôtel-Dieu and had her mother and brother arrested and brought to the nearest jail. Unable to stay in the room because of the putrid smell, the prosecutor broke the shutters open to air out the room. He put off the investigation until the next day.

When the investigators returned, they inspected Henriette Launier's room and found 43,000 francs in a metal box, along with her last will and a significant number of stocks and securities. They took note of the opulence in other areas of the mansion in contrast to the squalor of Blanche's room.

Inside Blanche's room, they read the inscriptions she had written on the walls:

Will I ever be free? Will I always be trapped in this jail cell? Will I ever be rescued?

Am I condemned to be buried alive in this tomb? My life is over!

Will I always be this unfortunate? Will I spend my whole life in isolation?

Freedom! Freedom! Always alone! I must live my whole life and die in this dark hole!

There are favorite children in some families.

A crowd soon formed in Rue de la Visitation, shouting with indignation and hostility. The maids who had been fired started to talk. The neighbors said they had heard Blanche's cries for help and that they believed she had been pregnant with Gilles Lomet's child but her parents had forced her to have an abortion. Tongues were wagging all over town.

All of France became obsessed with the case, and reporters arrived from every corner. It was a scandal! Since Henriette Launier was an ardent parishioner, rather than describe the horror that Blanche had endured, the Royalist newspapers jumped to the defense of her mother. It was as if they thought the Catholic Church itself were on trial. Républicain journalists used the case as a pretext to argue the other side, condemning Royalist Catholics.

For the vast majority of journalists, however, the girl's captivity was the story. *L'Avenir de la Vienne* summarized public opinion in their article dated October 6, 1901. They wrote:

"Is this a case of forced captivity or simply a case of neglect? The inscriptions written on the walls over twenty years ago testify to the fact that Blanche was deprived of her freedom, and the neighbors admit to having heard her cries for help. All this evidence certainly seems to prove that this is a case of illegal confinement."

Henriette Launier, who was very surprised to have been arrested for such a "trivial thing," disapproved of the menu options at the local jail. She had meals delivered to her from the restaurant at the Hôtel de France. Her favorite dish was chicken with peas in wine sauce. But her pride had been irreparably wounded. It could not withstand the scandal. Everyone was denouncing her actions. After two weeks in jail, fearing that she would be the next defendant on trial at the courthouse, her pride crushed her will to live, and she died.

To avoid the gathering of a hostile crowd, the funeral was held early in the morning in the prison chapel. But the crowd assembled anyway, amassing at dawn, and when the hearse exited the prison drive to take the body to its final resting place in the family plot at Chilvert cemetery, angry jeers erupted. Another enraged mob congregated at the gates to the cemetery, and the police had to be called to stop them from entering.

Meanwhile, Blanche was being cared for at the Hôtel-Dieu. The day she arrived, she weighed 25.5 kilograms, just over 56 pounds. By August, thanks to regular nutritious meals, she had put on an additional 10 kilograms. The doctor caring for her said that she had been rescued just in time. If she had stayed where she was any longer, she surely would have perished.

All anyone was talking about was the *"séquestrée de Poitiers,"* that poor woman held captive in Poitiers. The conservative newspapers argued that the only reason Blanche had been kept locked up all those years was because she was insane. It is interesting to note, however, that the three main people who cared for her at the Hôtel-Dieu—her nurse Sister Wilfred, her caretaker Amélie Raymond, and the hospital chaplain Father Mondion—all remarked publicly that their patient was very sweet and good-tempered.

In an article dated June 7 published in the newspaper *L'Éclair*, Father Mondion was quoted as saying the following: "I've said it once and I'll say it again: anyone who could leave a daughter, a sister, or even a stranger in the pitiful state that Mademoiselle Blanche was left in is a criminal, especially given the fact that the victim is a sweet, good, and calm person. Her windows are wide open, and we have seen no sign of her being irrational, hurtful, or dangerous. She is in a state of physical and mental depression, which is not surprising since she has spent so many years being deprived of fresh air and sunlight and was barely given any food to eat."

He repeated these words in public many times over the course of the whole affair, which went on for months: "Religion is not the issue here. There are warped individuals of every stripe, and I don't understand why Conservatives are trying to make excuses for Madame Launier's actions."

At the trial, Sister Wilfred said: "Not only does Blanche dislike being nude, which they claimed she preferred, she actually has shown signs of extreme modesty. When she gets out of bed, she wants everyone in the room to leave, and if someone wants to examine her legs, she always refuses to lift up her gown. She is extremely weak, but shows absolutely no signs of insanity."

It took several days, but Blanche got used to being in a clean bed and started to ask for the bedpan whenever she had to relieve herself.

Mademoiselle Amélie Raymond, who slept in the hospital room with her and was always by her side, told everyone that it was a true pleasure to care for her because Blanche was such a nice person.

At the end of May, after interviewing Blanche, a reporter from *L'Illustration* wrote: "It is hard to describe how ecstatic she is to have a new life, a clean bed, an open window through which she can see trees in the garden. She is starting to remember words, and her mind is getting sharper. She recognizes things that used to be familiar to her, types of flowers and birds. She finds everything amazing and enchanting. She is slowly learning to walk again. At first, her legs were so thin that she couldn't stand on her own. It's like a rebirth."

At fifty-two years old, surrounded by caring staff, Blanche started to speak again. Her first words were: "Oh, it's so nice here! You can see the sky!"

Epilogue

onoré Launier was brought before the Correctional Tribunal in Poitiers on October 7, 1901. He was not on trial for keeping Blanche captive—the person guilty of that was dead—but for his complicity on charges of unlawful assault and battery. The court limited its jurisdiction to the last three years in which Blanche was deemed mentally incapacitated. From the beginning to the end of the trial, there were record crowds at the courthouse. It was a real free-for-all as soon as the courtroom doors opened. Reporters came from all over France and from other countries, even Russia. The rest of the seats were filled primarily by women.

Evidence was exhibited on the left side of the courtroom. There were the shutters that had been busted open, the door to Blanche's room that had been broken and later repaired, the wood of the bed frame eaten away by vermin and rats, the straw mattress swarming with worms, the oilcloth on which she slept, jars full of lice, and her braid, one meter long, as stiff as wood and full of excrement, weighing over two kilograms. It all smelled terribly bad.

About one hundred witnesses were called to the stand, including former maids and neighbors who had heard Blanche's cries for help and, it should be noted, had done nothing to help. As people began to wonder about the complicity of the household staff, the maids made a point to declare that their boss had threatened to fire them if they said anything and to badmouth them to everyone in the city so that they would never be able to find work again, because she had a lot of influence in Poitiers.

Outside, in front of the Palais de Justice, as inside, you could hear wrathful jeers from the spectators. The defense lawyers tried to show that Honoré Launier was a respectful son and a weakling, incapable of standing up to his mother, that he had tried to get his mother to send Blanche to the hospital, but that his mother had slammed the door in his face and had partially disinherited him. To defend his client, Maître Barbier pushed his argument even further, so far that he ended up describing Honoré Launier, a former subprefect, as a bit of a moron. He exclaimed: "This man lacks the ability to see well, to smell well, and to fully comprehend anything."

The Correctional Tribunal was not convinced by the arguments of the defense. They concluded that the son was complicit in his passivity and that he had contributed to the harm done to his sister by Henriette Launier. In light of the authoritarian character of his mother, they declared that there were extenuating circumstances, and Honoré Launier was sentenced to only fifteen months in prison. When the verdict was announced, thunderous applause erupted in the courthouse.

Honoré Launier appealed the conviction, bolstered by the conservative bourgeoisie and Poitiers' most well-to-do families who all signed petitions asking the court to recognize his innocence. The judges heard the case again on November 20, 1901. This time, the court ruled that Honoré Launier's actions were indeed blameworthy, but that there was no law stating that passive complicity was a crime punishable by time in prison. The judges, unable to deem his actions illegal, acquitted Honoré Launier of his crimes. Public opinion found that justice had not been served, and the laws on this issue were later modified.

Blanche stayed in the Hôtel-Dieu until June of 1902. Her brother then took her away from Poitiers for good. After his trial, Honoré Launier had said that he would become his sister's guardian and manage her estate for her. He placed her in a convalescent home in Blois. Blanche died there in 1913.

In Poitiers, the only trace left of Blanche Launier were the words she had scribbled on the walls of her room and the faint echoes of her cries for freedom:

What have I done to be locked away and to suffer so? I do not deserve this torture. God must not exist if this is how his children are treated. Is there no one to protect me? Freedom! Freedom!

PHOTO ALBUM

1848: Letizia and Louis de Marcillat (Blanche's grandparents) and Henriette and Martin Launier (Blanche's parents) attended the trial and execution of Françoise Meunier and her son.

The last confession of the convict before his execution.

A public execution in the 19th century,
similar to that of Françoise Meunier and her son René.

Saint-Pierre Cathedral
Blanche was baptized in this cathedral by the bishop of Poitiers
on March 8, 1849.

The Poitiers train station, with coaches waiting to pick up trave-
lers. This train station was often used by the Launier family (trips
to Paris for Blanche's parents, trips to La Rochelle for Blanche and
her grandparents, various trips taken by her brother Honoré).

Main doors of Saint-Pierre Cathedral where Blanche received her
First Communion in 1861.

Entryway to Blossac Park, where Blanche used to go for walks
with her grandmother.

The shores along the Clain River, where Blanche and Gilles Lomet would go for walks together.

Another place Blanche and Gilles Lomet used to take walks: Blossac Park.

Place d'Armes and the Hôtel de Ville (City Hall), constructed in 1869, just steps away from Blanche's house.

The Hôtel de Ville in Poitiers, where numerous conflicts between Royalists and Républicains took place after the fall of the Second Empire.

The "new" Prefecture, where Honoré Launier worked, inaugurated in 1868.

Saint-Porchaire Church, where Henriette Launier attended mass later in her life.

Sainte-Radegonde Church, where people from Poitiers go to pray for salvation.

People praying to Saint Radegonde, as Henriette Launier wanted her daughter to do, to make her renounce her love for Gilles Lomet.

The house where Blanche was held captive
at 21 Rue de la Visitation
(today called Rue Arthur Ranc).

Two of Henriette Launier's maids. On the right is Prudence Renou, who helped to free Blanche by contacting Commissioner Bucheton.

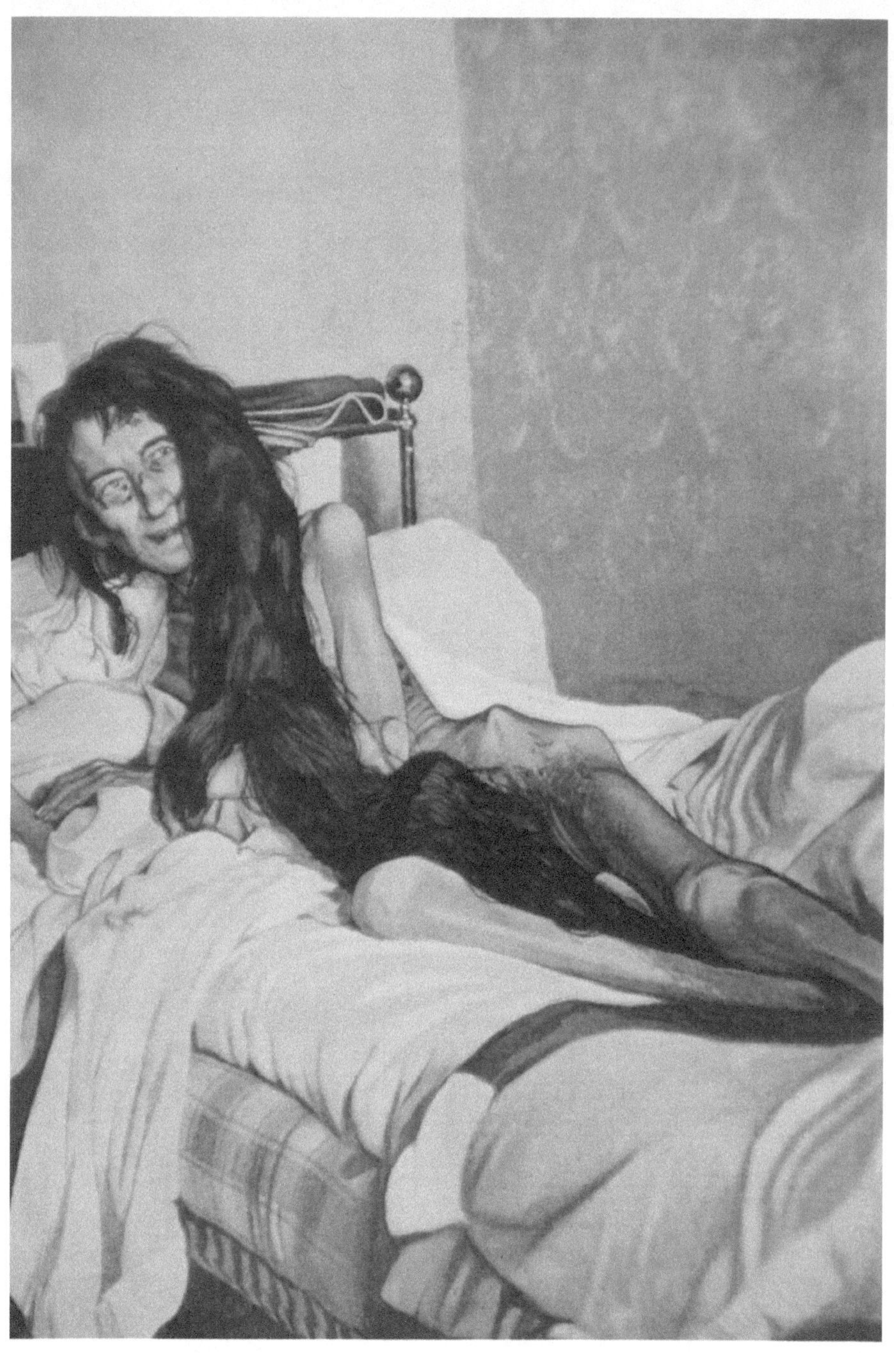

Blanche shortly after being admitted to the hospital;
she weighed 25.5 kilos (56 pounds).

Blanche in her room at the Hôtel-Dieu.

Entrance to the old prison on Rue de la Visitation, where
Henriette Launier was held and where she died.

In 1904, the old prison on
Rue de la Visitation was
replaced by this grand post
office. To the left is Rue des
Écossais, to the right is Rue
de la Visitation.

The Palais de Justice in Poitiers, where Honoré Launier was put on trial.

The entrance hall at the Palais de Justice in Poitiers, 1901.

The presiding judge.

The accused: Honoré Launier,
Blanche's brother.

Testimony given by Father
Mondion,
chaplain of the Hôtel-Dieu, who
cared for Blanche after she came
to the hospital.

Testimony of Prudence Renou (the new maid) who explained how she discovered that Blanche was being held captive and everything that she did to let people know about it.

Testimony of Bernadette Chaigneau, one of Henriette Launier's maids.

Testimony from one of the other maids who worked in Henriette Launier's household.

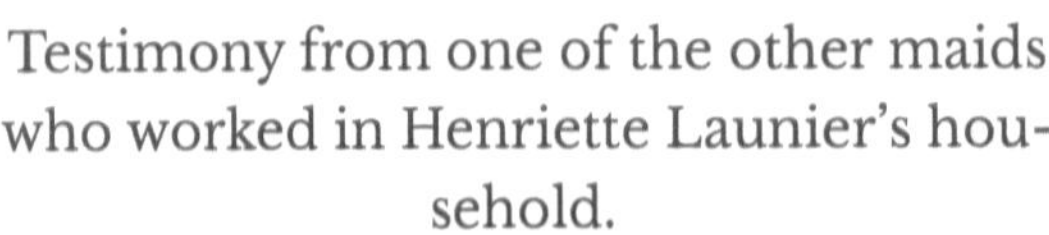

Photo of Father Mondion, who defended Blanche in all of the newspapers.

Sources

L'Avenir de la Vienne, May, June, July, September, October, and November 1901.

Le Courrier de la Vienne et des Deux-Sèvres, June, September, October, November 1901.

L'Illustration, May and October 1901.

La Croix, May and June 1901.

L'Écho de Paris, May and June 1901.

L'Univers, May and June 1901.

Le Petit Journal, May 1901.

L'Éclair, May 1901.

La Libre Parole, May and June 1901.

La Séquestrée de Poitiers. Observations de la défense adressées à la chambre des mises en accusation de la Cour d'appel de Poitiers, by M. E. Barbier, Poitiers, Société française d'imprimerie et de librairie, 1901.

Bibliography

Bouvier, Jean. *Les deux scandales de Panama. René Julliard*, 1964.

Chiron, Jean. *Voyage dans l'histoire de la Vienne.* Geste éditions, 1994.

Dansett, Adrien. *L'attentat d'Orsini.* Éditions Mondiales, 1964.

Duby, Georges. *Histoire de la France de 1852 à nos jours.* Références Larousse, 1987.

Favreau, Robert. *Poitiers.* Beauchesne, 1988.

Gide, André. *Ne jugez pas.* Gallimard, 1930.

Histoire de Poitiers. Privat, 1985.

Lachnitt, Jean-Claude. *Le Prince impérial Napoléon IV*. Perrin, 1997.

Les grandes heures de la Troisième République. Librairie Académique Perrin, 1967.

L'Histoire du Poitou Protestant. Éditions Maison du Protestantisme Poitevin, 1994.

Protestants de l'Ouest 1517-1987. Éditions Ouest-France, 1993.

Contents

BY THE SAME AUTHOR

Couple criminel, Ian Brady—Myra Hindley, *3E éditions,* 2021.

Le juge de Dieu Nicolas Rémy, ses sorciers et ses sorcières, *3E éditions,* 2020.

L'ogre de la gare d'Hanovre, l'affaire Haarmann, *3E éditions,* 2019.

Un marquis si pieux, l'affaire de Nayve, *3E éditions,* 2018.

Trois saisons en enfer, les possédées de Loudun, *Geste éditions,* 2017.

Le grenier magique, *Geste éditions,* 2016.

Petites Angevines en danger, *éditions du Petit Pavé,* 2015.

Ils sont venus pour nous, Joseph Boczov et Olga Bancic, *3E éditions,* 2016, *éditions L'àpart,* 2013.

Le double visage du Dr Karl Roos, Nid d'espions en Alsace-Lorraine, *3E éditions,* 2016, *éditions L'àpart,* 2012.

Les Diaboliques de Waldighoffen, *3E éditions* 2020, *éd. du Bout de la rue,* 2011.

Le tueur du Paris-Mulhouse, 3E éditions 2017, *éditions L'àpart,* 2010.

Une vierge assassinée, 3E éditions 2017, *Cheminements* 2009.

Puissances démoniaques en terre maçonne, *3E éditions,* 2017, *éditions Cheminements,* 2008.

L'empoisonneuse à la digitaline, *3E éditions,* 2016, *éditions Cheminements,* 2007.

L'enfant assassin, François 12 ans, *3E éditions,* 2017, *éditions Cheminements,* 2006.

Le crime de l'Ascension, *3E éditions,* 2017, *éd. Cheminements,* 2005

Le meurtrier du mois d'août, Marseil Sabourin, *3E éditions,* 2017, *éditions Cheminements,* 2004.

La Serpe du Maudit, Le roman de Pierre Rivière, *3E éditions,* 2017, *éditions Cheminements,* 2003.

Henri Pranzini, le Chéri magnifique, *3E éditions,* 2017, *éditions L'àpart,* 2012, *éditions Cheminements,* 2002.

La Séquestrée de Poitiers, Une affaire judiciaire sans précédent, *3E éditions,* 2015, *L'àpart* : 2012, *Cheminements* : 2001.

Suicide, modes de prévention, *éditions Isabelle Quentin,* Montréal, 1999.

Sida, Famille et Société, *L'Harmattan,* Paris, 1996.

Official author's website: janouin-benanti.com

ABOUT THE AUTHOR

With a background in law, politics, and public health, Viviane Janouin-Benanti spent many years working with community outreach organizations in France. Her first two books are related to her work in that field.

Today, Janouin-Benanti devotes her time exclusively to writing novels. Fascinated by true stories, her aim is to breathe life into her characters: real people who were the perpetrators and victims at the center of major criminal and historical cases. Her novels open the door for readers to peek into the personal lives of those involved in the crimes.

These works of creative nonfiction revive a centuries-long French tradition of retelling the stories of criminal cases. Based on true facts, they portray the realities of France's history, which was often tumultuous, vulnerable to regime changes, and rife with religious and social conflict. Viviane Janouin-Benanti dives deeply into her research to analyze the facts of each case, the motivations of key figures in the crimes, and other circumstances that may have contributed to the tragic events of each transgression. The human beings she describes are often very complex, and she does not try to simplify them. Through her study of court cases and the cultural contexts in which they occurred, she brings actual men and women back to life and tells their stories.

Viviane Janouin-Benanti also offers speaking engagements and lectures on the cases described in her novels. She has been interviewed about her books on numerous television and radio shows both in France and in Canada.

Website: janouin-benanti.com

ABOUT THE TRANSLATOR

Elizabeth Blood is a freelance translator based in the United States. With a Ph.D. in French literature and a long career as a professor of French, she is passionate about language and its ability to connect people across cultures.

E-mail: eblood@savoirfairetranslations.com

Website: https://savoirfairetranslations.com/

www.ingramcontent.com/pod-product-compliance
Lightning Source LLC
LaVergne TN
LVHW091700190726
843493LV00001B/75